HANDY REFERENCE

GW00597434

When you get your Internet connection set up, fill in this sheet to remind you details of your account. Then, if you need to upgrade any software in future, you've got all the details at your fingertips.

Warning: A box for your password is provided here. However, it is better if you can remember your password, but if you can't, <u>beware of prying eyes</u>. You have been warned.

Your Provider

Provider's Name:

Help Line Telephone Number:

Dial-up Number(s):

Help Line eMail Address:

DNS Server Address:

Your Account

Your Account Name:

Password **(careful!)**:

Your eMail Address:

eMail

Your Mail Server Address:

News

Your News Server Address:

World-Wide Web

Your Home Page: Port:

Proxy Server Address (if any):   Port:

ABOUT THE SERIES

In easy steps series is developed for time-sensitive people who want results fast. It is designed for quick, easy and effortless learning.

By using the best authors in the field, combined with our in-house expertise in computing, this series is ideal for all computer users. It explains the essentials simply, concisely and clearly - without the unnecessary verbal blurb. We strive to ensure that each book is technically superior, effective for easy learning and offers the best value.

Learn the essentials **in easy steps** - accept no substitutes!

Titles in the series include:

Operating Systems
Windows 95	1-874029-28-8

Applications - Integrated
Microsoft Office	1-874029-37-7
Microsoft Office 97	1-874029-66-0
Microsoft Works	1-874029-41-5
SmartSuite (97)	1-874029-67-9

Applications - General
Access	1-874029-57-1
Excel	1-874029-69-5
PowerPoint	1-874029-63-6
Word	1-874029-39-3
Word 97	1-874029-68-7
WordPerfect	1-874029-59-8

Accounting and Finance
Microsoft Money UK	1-874029-61-X
Quicken UK	1-874029-71-7
Sage Instant Accounting	1-874029-44-X
Sage Sterling for Windows	1-874029-43-1

Internet
CompuServe UK	1-874029-33-4
FrontPage	1-874029-60-1
HTML	1-874029-46-6
Internet Explorer	1-874029-58-X
Internet UK	1-874029-73-3
Netscape Navigator	1-874029-47-4

Graphics and Desktop Publishing
CorelDRAW	1-874029-72-5
PageMaker	1-874029-35-0
PagePlus	1-874029-49-0
Publisher	1-874029-56-3

Development Tools
Visual Basic	1-874029-74-1
Visual J++	1-874029-75-X

Hardware
Upgrading Your PC	1-874029-76-8

For credit card sales and volume discounts Tel: 01926 817999 or EMail: sales@computerstep.com

For international orders and rights Fax: +44 1926 817005 or EMail: sevanti@computerstep.com

EMail your reader comments to: harshad@computerstep.com

Visit our web site at http://www.computerstep.com

INTERNET UK
in easy steps

Andy Holyer

COMPUTER STEP

In easy steps is an imprint of Computer Step
Southfield Road . Southam
Warwickshire CV33 OFB . England

Tel: 01926 817999 Fax: 01926 817005
http://www.computerstep.com

Second edition published 1997
First published 1996

Notice of Liability
Every effort has been made to ensure that this book contains accurate
and current information. However, Computer Step and the author
shall not be liable for any loss or damage suffered by readers as a
result of any information contained herein.

Trademarks
Microsoft® and Windows® are registered trademarks of Microsoft
Corporation. All other trademarks are acknowledged as belonging to
their respective companies.

Printed and bound in the United Kingdom

ISBN 1-874029-73-3

Contents

6. File Transfer Protocol 109

7. Telnet 117

8. Internet Relay Chat 123

First Steps

This chapter explains the basic concepts of the Internet, and the various things you'll need to get started.

Covers

A Brief History

The Internet is a "network of networks" which connects together computers all over the world. These computers range from Supercomputers to PCs: it is estimated that there are about 40 million people connected, and that number is increasing by 10% per quarter.

The origins of the Internet lie in the Cold War. A plan was devised to connect up military computers spread around the United States, so that in case of nuclear attack the US military machine would still be able to operate. These machines were linked together using telephone lines. The first two machines were connected up at the end of 1969.

For the first 15 years of its life, almost the only sites connected were military and academic. There were a number of networks set up: ARPAnet, which connected US universities: MILnet, which connected up military bases. The first UK system linked up five UK universities in the late seventies. This grew into the UK academic network, JANET.

In the 1980s the various networks began to be linked together, so you could get from one network to another. This is when the name "Internet" was first coined.

The first public on-line services appeared in the late seventies - CompuServe was the best known, but this has only been connected to the Internet in the last few years. A similar system was Britain's CIX, which started in the late eighties. Britain's first real public Internet service was Demon Internet, which began in 1989, and is still one of the biggest. Since 1994 over 200 new Internet Providers have started up in the UK.

How a Connection Happens

Physically, most Internet connections use telephone lines, whether they are high-speed digital leased lines, or the ordinary telephone line into your house.

You telephone from your computer to your Internet provider. The provider's computers use a high-speed leased line to faster connections, on what is called the "backbone". The computers on the backbone use very high-speed connections to connect to other backbone links, possibly in other countries. These foreign backbone links connect in turn to local providers, and from there on to the individual foreign machines.

All data that you send on the Internet is divided into chunks of about 256 bytes, called "packets". Each packet is marked with the address from which it came, and the address to which it is going. This is how the backbone systems know where to send them.

You don't need to know exactly which route each packet takes; the backbone will ensure that they go by whatever is the most convenient route at the time. It is even possible for different packets to go by different routes.

At the other end the packets are put back together again to form the original data.

Packet switching (as this process is called) allows more than one person to share a single line at one time - as long as all the packets arrive at the other end, the message still gets through. One of the odd things you'll find when you connect to the Internet is that it's possible for you to send or receive several different things at once over a single modem link - the speed of the connection is just divided down.

The rules on how the data is broken down into packets, and how the packets are addressed, is called a "protocol". The protocol used by the Internet is called "TCP/IP". This stands for Transmission Control Protocol/Internet Protocol.

Modems

Unless your connection to the Internet is via a Local-Area-Network provided by a company or university, you will use a modem to connect to the Internet.

A modem can be thought of as an answering machine for your computer. It connects to a COM port of your computer (either by means of a cable, or by providing its own COM port, modem and port plugging into a single expansion slot). The other end of the modem is a cable ending in a telephone plug, which you put in a normal telephone socket just as you would for a fax or an answering machine. The modem takes in computer signals from the COM port and converts them ("modulates" them) into tones which it sends down the telephone line to another modem on the other end, which converts them back ("demodulates" them). The word "modem" is short for "modulator-demodulator".

A modem does not need a special telephone socket, though you should bear a few things in mind. The sockets of some office switchboard systems do not allow a modem to be plugged in - though you can't tell from looking at the socket. These switchboards use what are sometimes called "system" phones, which often have all sorts of extra buttons, displays etc. Switchboards are worth avoiding in any case, since they tend to do other odd things to modem connections, such as not giving what the modem thinks is a dial tone, or hanging up the phone at various times (the switchboard sends pulses down the line to check if the phone is in use, which a human won't notice, but which makes the modem think the other end has rung off). If you're in a situation like this, the best solution (assuming you can't just install an extra direct line) is to share the fax machine's telephone line (you can simply use a normal 2-way phone adapter, available for £1 or so from shops that sell telephones). The only disadvantage of this scheme is that your company's fax appears to be busy while you're on-line.

A call to an Internet provider is going to be quite long as telephone calls go (an hour or two is not unusual), so it's worth doing what you can to make sure that the calls are as cheap as possible. If you buy your telephone service from a cable television company, they often provide cheap or even free calls: if you don't live in the right area for this, it's worth investigating BT's "Friends and Family" scheme, which allows you to specify a list of numbers (including your Internet provider) to which calls are much cheaper.

Modems come in a range of makes and models, and the range can be quite bewildering. Any modem you buy nowadays should be "Hayes compatible", which describes the system of instructions you send to the modem to get it to dial, etc. It's not really worth buying a very old modem, (over 5 years old), but if you should, make sure that it is Hayes compatible.

Unless you're *really* short of cash, the lowest specification modem you should consider is one which handles the "V34" standard - which means that it will send and receive data at up to 28,800 bits per second. If you already have a 14,400 modem, that will work fine, but it's not really worth buying one - they are only about £30 cheaper, and you'll soon use up the difference in cost in increased on-line time.

You should expect to pay between £120 and £200 for a V34 modem. If you can afford it, consider investing in a 33,600 baud modem. They cost about an extra £50, and not all Internet service providers can support them, but they are even faster than a 28,800.

There is a new modem standard just coming out as I write this, which provides up to 56K connections; it does this by only providing the highest speed on the download link - that is, from your provider to you. Since most people do collect more data from the Internet than they send to it, this is not really a problem. Check if your provider can handle these modems before committing the extra cash, and bear in mind that you need a very clear telephone line to get full speeds out of them. If you live out in the country, or if your

HANDY TIP

On any telephone line, it's worth making sure that any "star services" are turned off - especially Call Waiting, which can also cause the modem to hang up at odd moments. BT will send you a nice little leaflet describing how to turn these services off before you use the modem, and how to turn them on again after you ring off.

house has old telephone lines, or even if your local telephone exchange has not yet been upgraded, you will not get full speed out of high-speed modems. If any of these are the case, you may not be able to connect at 28,800 even if you buy a higher speed modem.

There is a wide variety of modems on the market. Good brands include U.S. Robotics, Motorola, Hayes, and Psion (their "Surfer" modem has been widely advertised). There is also a bewildering collection of no-name brands available at a cheaper price. It is possible with a bit of tweaking to get as good results from a no-name modem as with a more expensive brand; however, if you have problems, your Internet provider will be more likely to be able to help if you have a more well-known model. Some of the more expensive models of modem (for instance the US Robotics Courier) allow you to upgrade them using a software patch which you can download from the Internet; with a cheaper model, your only choice is to buy a new modem and try and sell your old one. For years I used a US Robotics Sportster with no trouble at all; for the last year I have had a Motorola 3400 which has been equally reliable.

Internal Modems

You can buy internal modems for PCs. These come as either an expansion card which you plug into a PC slot, or as a PCMCIA card for a laptop.

Internal modems have a number of advantages: they cut down the number of boxes you have on your desk, they cut down the number of cables and main sockets, and, perhaps most importantly, they are about £10 cheaper than external modems.

Some people are very keen on internal modems. I'm not so keen, for one reason: one of the best ways to check that everything's working properly is to look at the lights on the modem. Internal modems don't have status lights, so you lose a useful diagnostic tool. Once they're going, however, internal modems are a neat solution.

Internet Providers

If you work for a large corporation, or are at a university, your connection to the Internet will be a direct one - your computer is permanently connected. The rest of us, however, have to rely on a dial-up connection, and the company who provides this is called an Internet Service Provider.

Internet providers run a computer system which is permanently connected to the Internet, and which, more importantly, runs the banks of modems which subscribers use to dial in (this is referred to as a "modem farm" in the trade). Providers also run server systems for the various services found on the Internet - in particular, they run a World-Wide Web server, which often provides information about their area, and special resources for their subscribers.

There are several hundred Internet service providers in the UK, with more appearing all the time. With this in mind, it would be pointless to recommend any particular provider - any suggestions would be out of date before the book went to print. I can, however, give some general guidelines.

Internet providers charge a subscription of between £7 and £20 per month. It sometimes works out cheaper if you pay a year in advance rather than monthly. The difference in price between the most and the least expensive services is less important than it may at first appear. You need to take into account your potential telephone bills as well - and that will be a lot more than £10 per month. It's difficult to generalise, but a cheap service is often going to result in engaged tones at evenings and weekends (they have less cash to spend on extra dial-in lines); there's no point getting a cheap connection if you can never connect when you want to.

There is no such thing as a perfect service provider; all of them are good for some people, bad for others. No provider, large or small, has ever managed a perfect service - there will always be times when there is a breakdown, and you can't collect your mail.

Make sure that the provider you are thinking about has a Point of Presence (a dial-in number) within a local call of you. Some small providers have just a single PoP; if that is in your own town, and you don't expect to need to connect when you are away, that could be just what you need. You will get the advantage of local support (no long-distance calls to the help desk), and other people on the same service will often live near you, and will be interested in similar issues. Some local providers have phone lines supplied by their local cable provider; if you can buy your modem phone line from the same company, this can mean that you can dial in for free at off-peak times.

Larger ISPs cover the whole country, either by having a network of Points of Presence, or by using a local-call number. This can be useful if you use a laptop, and are likely to want to collect your eMail when you are away from home. With a large company, the support software is likely to be better quality, but getting support can be more tricky if you have problems.

You may be tempted by the free trial disks which online services like CompuServe, AOL and MSN hand out. These services are not "real" Internet connections; you can get access to the 'Net, but the real point of them is access to the added-value service which they carry. For example, if you subscribe to CompuServe, you can have computer banking with TSB. Most of these on-line services charge a low monthly fee, but then charge per minute of connect time after an hour or two per month. Some added-value services also charge each time you use them. Be careful; these extra charges can work out very expensive, and can be a nasty shock when your monthly bill arrives. Unless your on-line time is very low, or you have a specific need for an added-value service, a conventional ISP will work out cheaper.

Remember, by the way, that there's no law to say that you can only have one account; I run three, for different purposes.

Choosing an Internet Provider

As I said before, it's pointless giving particular recommendations in a book, since the Internet Provider market is so volatile. The best way to find yourself a provider is to look in one of the many Internet magazines, which all provide a complete listing. These are the things you should look for in an Internet provider:

Points of Presence
The locations to which subscribers can ring in are called Points of Presence, or PoPs for short. Some providers have only one PoP; some have a number. Since the largest single cost you will face in using the Internet is your telephone bill, it's very important that you choose a provider who has a PoP as close to you as possible.

Modem Ratio
The standard rule of thumb to determine how easy it will be to get through to a provider is to look at the ratio of the number of subscribers to the number of modems in the provider's PoPs. The industry standard ratio is 30:1 - any provider who can't manage this should be treated with suspicion. Many providers aim for a much lower ratio - 20:1 is OK, 15:1 is good. The ratio can change almost from week to week, so it's worth asking the provider what the current ratio is. Also, beware of a new provider: these can often boast very low ratios - 4:1 even - but these ratios will drop rapidly as the number of subscribers rises. The acid test is how high the ratio rises before the provider can upgrade their PoPs.

Software Provided
The software which a provider supplies you with can vary widely, as can the way it's supplied. In this book I'll describe the standard software which will work with most providers; as they say on the Internet, "Your mileage may vary". A package of commercial Internet software will cost at least £50: some providers supply this, which can explain a high initial registration fee. Remember, by the way, that you can usually run commercial software with most providers, if you so wish.

Signing up

There are a couple of things you should think about before you sign up with a provider. The most important one to consider is the account name you would like.

Providers differ in their approach to account names. Some just assign you a name, with no choice involved. Others allow you more-or-less a free choice, as long as the name has not already been used. Often there are restrictions on your choice: account names are usually lower-case only, with no spaces, and they are often restricted to 8 characters.

HANDY TIP

Providers often have their own preferred naming styles - it's worth asking them before you commit to a different way.

There are a number of different approaches to choosing an address. Remember, your account name will often become your eMail address, so this is the way you will appear to the rest of the world. An account name like "bambi" may seem cute at first thought, but it is possible that you'll think a bit differently in five years time when you're using eMail to apply for a job.

Besides the silly names (don't even bother to ask for names like "spock" - you can bet your life someone's already asked for it), there are two or three common approaches to making an eMail address out of a name. It's worth following these, since they're accepted as "normal" on the Internet.

The one I use is "given name followed by first letter(s) of surname". Thus, my account name is "andyh". Had there already been an "andyh" on the system, I'd have been "andyho". Another approach is to just use your surname. This is fine for me, but less useful if your name is "Smith". Yet another is "initial-surname", which would make me "aholyer".

Most providers take a fairly dim view of people who want to change their eMail address after their account is set up. A few minutes of thought beforehand can avoid a lot of hassle later.

Internet Software

There is a wide variety of software available to help you access the Internet. When you sign up with your chosen provider, they should supply you with programs to handle each of the services available. If you like the programs they supply, fine - you'll get the best support from them if you use the setup they provide.

However, for each service on the Internet there are several different applications available. Assuming you're using a genuine Internet service provider (that is, not a proprietary on-line service like CompuServe) then you're quite at liberty to use whichever programs you like. It's worth experimenting to find out which packages suit you best.

Most Internet software is available for download direct from the Internet. Most of this is freeware or shareware. You also often find Internet packages on the cover disks of computer magazines. There are glossy shrink-wrapped packages available in the shops, but this software is not necessarily better than the stuff available for free.

HANDY TIP

For details of where to find the software discussed in this book, see Chapter 10.

Because there is such a wide range of software available, it's impossible for me to predict exactly which setup you'll be using. In this book I describe the most often used freeware or shareware packages. All the software I describe is available for download from the Internet - that's how I got hold of it - so with a little patience you will be able to duplicate my setup. If you prefer other packages, that's fine. Besides going through the buttons and menus of each package, I've tried to explain how each service works, so that if you use a different item of software you'll not be entirely at sea.

Internet software usually consists of a package which handles your connection to your provider, and runs the SLIP or PPP protocols you use to connect yourself to the Internet, and one application for each Internet service. In general, it's OK to mix and match these programs as you wish - you can even have more than one package of the same type installed at once, so that you can compare them.

ISDN

A faster method of connection to the Internet is by using an ISDN (Integrated Services Digital Network) telephone line. An ISDN line is a special telephone connection which you can order from BT. A normal telephone line is analogue - that is, it carries a varying voltage to convey speech or data. An ISDN line is digital, like the signals inside your computer. Because it is digital, an ISDN line can carry a great deal more data; a single line gives you access to two channels, each of which can carry either voice or data at up to 64 kilobaud.

An ISDN line costs (at the time of writing) £199 to install. BT will take about a month to install your line, and installation is dependent on the quality of the lines between your house or office and your local exchange; you may find that it is impossible to install ISDN in some areas.

Since ISDN is digital, you don't need a modem; instead you use a device called a "Terminal Adapter" or "TA" for short. A TA will cost about £300, and looks and acts as far as you are concerned exactly like a modem - you connect it to your ISDN socket, and via a serial cable to your computer, and use the same software as you would for a modem - except faster.

Most TAs also have two telephone sockets where you can plug in an ordinary phone, a fax, or even an analogue modem (if you want to). You can connect to the Internet over an ISDN line, and still make or receive calls on one of the two analogue lines at the same time. Alternatively, you can have both analogue lines operating at once.

If you want to assign the two telephone points on your TA to different numbers (say to make one your phone line and one your fax line) then you also need to subscribe to another BT service called "Multiple Subscriber Numbering" or MSN for short. This costs an extra £10 per quarter, and gives you a block of ten numbers, of which you can assign one to each analogue port. You could have another TA connected to your ISDN line, and give that two other numbers, working as a neat little office switchboard at a low cost.

I have connected to the Internet using an ISDN line for the past few months, and I am very pleased with it. Some services are very fast - collecting mail goes at a great speed, and Web pages can appear almost instantly. You do still find yourself waiting for some pages to appear, though: the Internet is only as fast as the slowest link in the chain, and some sites will still appear at 100 bytes per second, even over ISDN.

If you have a network of computers which you wish to connect to the Internet, it may be worth investing in an ISDN router. This is a box which costs about £1,000 (though some Internet providers will rent one to you instead). It is connected to your local area network, and to an ISDN line, and any time anyone tries to fetch data from outside of your network, the router will dial up your provider. The user then has a 64k connection to the Internet, without having to go through all the business of dialling in. When nobody is using the line for a period of time, the router hangs up, to save your telephone bill. Apart from a small delay if the router has to dial up, the Internet and the local network appear as one big network. A local area connection with a provider usually costs more than a normal dial-up connection, but can work out cheaper than giving everyone their own modem and phone line.

Bonding

An ISDN line allows you two connections at once; these could both be digital connections. Some providers allow "bonding", which allows you to dial in on both lines at once (paying two phone charges), and so get 128K out of an ISDN. Check with your provider if you are interested in trying this - it can be quite tricky to set up.

Cable Modems

There is a new technology which some of the cable television providers promise to introduce during 1997. Using a cable modem, your uplink connection (from you to the Internet) uses a modem as usual, while the downlink (from the Internet to your computer) comes directly down a fibre optic cable. This means that your apparent connection to the Internet is at local-area network speeds - up to 500K is possible.

No cable provider in the UK currently provides this service, so it is impossible to say how much it will cost.

There is a similar service available, called DirecPC, which uses a satellite dish to download data. You need to buy a special dish and PC card (costing £1,150 + VAT), and pay a monthly subscription to the service (either £15 or £52 per month depending on how much data you wish to download). You also need to have a normal modem link to an Internet provider.

You dial in to your provider as usual, and send requests just as you would in a normal dial-up service. Incoming data is delivered from satellite, at a claimed 400 thousand bits per second.

Personally, I'm not impatient enough to pay *that* much for a fast Internet service (and there's still a doubt as to whether all sites would arrive at 400K even using this system). If you are interested, the DirecPC service is available in America and Europe between the tropic of Cancer and the Arctic Circle. Look at

`http://www.direcpc.com`

for details of the service; a UK dealer can be found at

`http://www.sat-dig.co.uk`

If anyone tries it, let me know how you get on!

CHAPTER TWO

Getting Your Connection

This chapter explains how to set up Windows to connect to the Internet, and describes some of the problems you may encounter.

Covers

Getting Started

To connect to the Internet, you need a personal computer and a modem. I am assuming in this book that your PC runs Windows 95 or above. The software you need to dial in and to connect to the Internet is included on the Windows CD (or floppies) which came with your computer. If you do not have your original CD, then you can get the software (and some other useful applications) in the Microsoft Windows extras pack, available from most software dealers.

If your computer runs Windows 3.1 or 3.11, you will need some other software, which your Internet provider should supply.

If your computer does not run Windows, it's probably worth upgrading. There is Internet software which operates under DOS, but it is much lower quality, comes with no support, and is really for experts only.

A Windows machine should have at least 8Mb of memory to run the programs to access the Internet. If you have 16Mb or more, things will run much faster. This is more than you need for word-processing and suchlike because when you are connected to the Internet you need to run several applications at once, and this requires more computer resources.

Many of the "Multimedia PCs" which you can buy in the shops arrive already fitted with a modem. If not, you will need to buy one. If you don't already have a second phone line in your house, it is worth buying one: it is easy to tie up the phone for an hour or two at a time when using the Internet, and a dedicated modem line will make you much more popular with the other members of your household!

You will also need an account with an Internet service provider; I have discussed the options for this in Chapter One. Your Windows PC contains all the software to connect you to Microsoft's own service, MSN; this is not a bad choice, but it is not the cheapest option. Shop around, before you sign up with MSN.

Connection Software

Internet software can be divided into two types. There are the various application programs which you use to send and receive electronic mail, browse the World-Wide Web and access news. I will look at these in their own chapters.

The other type of Internet software is less interesting, but is important to get working properly. This is the software which controls your modem, dials in to your Internet service provider, sends your account details, and then lets your computer send and receive data using the protocol used by the Internet, TCP/IP. This software allows TCP/IP to work over telephone lines, SLIP (Serial Line IP) and PPP (Point-to-Point Protocol).

If you are using Windows 95 or above, it is best to use the TCP/IP and PPP packages which come with the operating system. If your computer uses Windows 3.1 or 3.11, you will need to use a program called Trumpet Winsock which does the same thing.

You can use Trumpet under later versions of Windows, but it is better to use the Microsoft package if you can get it to work. The Windows 95 software is a 32-bit application, which means it runs more quickly with less load on your machine than Trumpet, which is 16-bit. Some software, such as recent versions of Netscape and Microsoft Internet Explorer, will only work with a 32-bit TCP/IP program.

If you need to use Trumpet, you should be able to get it from your Internet provider (it usually comes on the setup disks which they supply). Trumpet is shareware, which means that it is free for you to use for one month. After that, you should register it, which costs 25 Australian dollars - about £12.

A Typical Internet Session

Each time you connect to the Internet, you should go through these steps:

1 Use your TCP/IP software to connect in to your Internet provider. For the rest of your session, you are making a telephone call to your provider (and running up a phone bill).

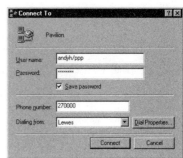

2 Minimize your TCP/IP software (if necessary) but do not quit it - that would disconnect you from the Internet.

HANDY TIP **Many tasks can be performed off-line to save the phone bill – e.g. reading and composing eMail, reading News, etc...**

3 Run your Internet applications - read electronic mail, browse the Web, read news. You can even run several applications at the same time.

When you have finished using the Internet, continue as follows:

4 Tell your TCP/IP software to disconnect. Using Windows 95, you do this by clicking on the "connection" icon…

5 And then click on the "Disconnect" button.

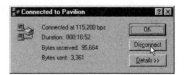

Setting up TCP/IP Software

If your computer has Windows installed just as it came out
of the box (that is, you haven't deleted any icons off the
desktop), you should have an icon labelled "The Internet"
sitting on your desktop. If this is the case, then you're
lucky; there is a Wizard which will set up TCP/IP for your
modem and Internet service provider.

1 Click on the icon "The Internet".

2 You will see the
Wizard start.
Click "Next".

3 There are three
options on the
next screen. If
you choose
"Automatic" you
will be set up to
use the Microsoft
Network; if you
want to use a
different ISP,
choose "Manual".
Then click
"Next".

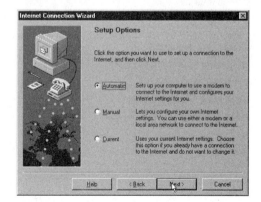

...contd

4 Unless you use a
company LAN for
your connection to
the Internet, you
should select
"Connect using my
phone line"

**In Chapter
Four, I
describe
using
Eudora for eMail,
which is more
powerful than
Microsoft's
package. I suggest
you select "No"
here.**

5 If you want to use
Microsoft's software
for electronic mail,
select "Yes"; if you
would prefer to use a
different package,
select "No".

**You may
be asked
to insert
one of
your Windows
master disks (either
a floppy or the CD),
so that Windows
can find the modem
driver software.**

6 Windows should
have detected your
modem when you
plugged it in. If so, it
should show it here.
If not, select it from
the list.

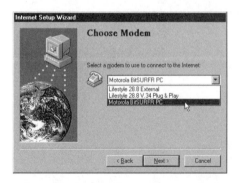

7 Type the name of
your Internet
Service Provider
into the box in the
next screen.

8 Your provider should tell you the phone number of their local Point of Presence. Type this into the next box.

REMEMBER

With some providers you may find that you have to put "/ppp" after your user name so that the computer on the other end knows to use PPP. Your provider should tell you if this is necessary.

9 Your provider should have told you your user name and password. Fill them in the box.

10 With almost all ISPs, you should keep the first option set. A few (Demon Internet is the only one I know of) assign you your very own IP address. If this is the case, select the second option and fill in the box.

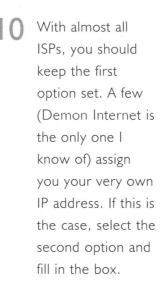

...contd

The Domain Name Service (DNS) is a computer which converts full Internet addresses (such as "computerstep.com") into the numerical form which Internet applications use. You have to know the numerical version of this address - it will be four numbers with dots between them.

11 Your provider should have told you the address of their Domain Name Server. Fill this in the box. If there is a secondary server, fill this in, too.

12 Click Finish. That's it! You are now set up to connect to the Internet.

Setting up TCP/IP by hand

There's a possibility that you are unlucky, and you do not have the Internet Connection Wizard installed on your PC. In this case, you can do the same thing using the Control Panel:

Open the "Control Panel" window (you can find it in the "Settings" section of the Windows "Start" menu). Double-click the "Add/Remove Programs" icon.

2 Select the "Windows Setup" tab.

3 Select the "Communications" option.

4 Click on "Details".

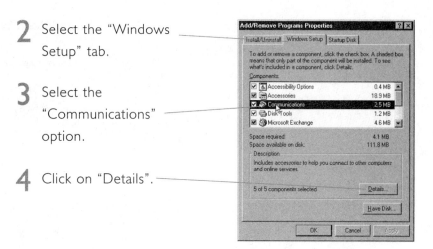

HANDY TIP

Windows will ask you to insert your installation disks or CD - make sure you have them handy!

5 If the "Dial-Up Networking" option is not selected, select it and click "OK".

6 In the Control Panel window, double-click on the "Network" icon. You should see both "Dial-Up Adapter" and "TCP/IP" in the list. If either is missing, you should add them:

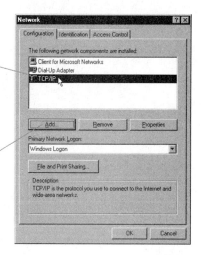

7 Click on "Add".

8 To add the Dial-up
   Adapter, double-click
   on "Adapter". To add
   TCP/IP, click on
   "Protocol". Then click
   the "Add" button.

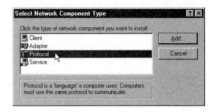

9 In either case, select
   "Microsoft", then
   either "Dial-Up
   Adapter" or "TCP/
   IP". Click "OK".

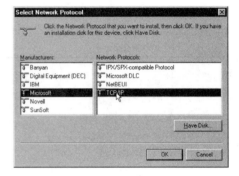

10 Back in the "Network"
    window, double-click
    on "TCP/IP".

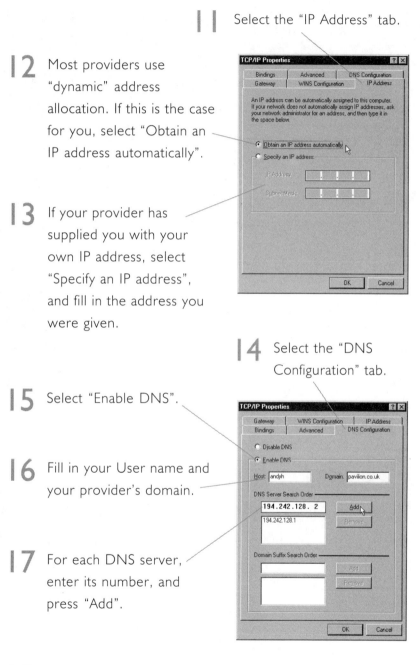

11 Select the "IP Address" tab.

12 Most providers use "dynamic" address allocation. If this is the case for you, select "Obtain an IP address automatically".

13 If your provider has supplied you with your own IP address, select "Specify an IP address", and fill in the address you were given.

14 Select the "DNS Configuration" tab.

15 Select "Enable DNS".

16 Fill in your User name and your provider's domain.

17 For each DNS server, enter its number, and press "Add".

18 Click "OK" to close the Networking Control Panel. Windows will ask to reboot your computer. Do so.

19 Now you need to set up your connection icon. Double-click on "My Computer", then double-click on "Dial-Up Networking".

20 Double-click on "Make New Connection". This will run a Wizard to set up your connection.

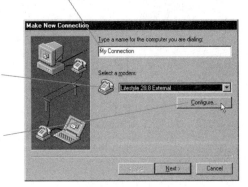

21 Fill in a name for your connection.

22 Select your modem type (Plug and Play may have done this for you).

23 Select "Configure".

24 Set the appropriate settings for your modem. In particular, set the connection speed to as fast as possible - at least 38400, and it's worth trying to see if 115,200 will work.

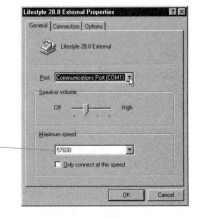

25 Click "OK", then "Next" to go to the next screen.

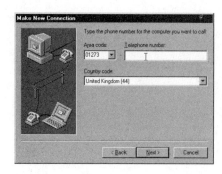

26 Type in the phone number of the connection.

27 That's it! You will now have an icon in Dial-Up Networking for your new connection. To connect, simply double-click this icon.

Troubleshooting

Despite following the instructions, you may still find that things don't work. Don't panic: setting things up the first time is the worst - once you've got everything going it should be fine from then on. Here are some possible problems:

Your modem does nothing

Assuming you use an external modem, this suggests that there is something wrong with the serial connection to the modem.

1 Check that the serial cable is firmly in its socket (and in the right socket!).

2 Make sure that your serial is a "Hardware Handshaking" cable. This has all 25 pins on each plug connected together. Some cheap serial cables save money on cable by only connecting four of the pins together. These will *not* work reliably for a high-speed Internet link. It's worth trying a different cable (most shops which sell computers have them for about £5).

3 Try reducing the connection speed until you get a response. Some very old computers could only manage 19,200 baud. In this case you need a new serial card (or a new computer!).

The provider's system refuses your password

Check that your user name and password are *exactly* as your provider has specified. Both user name and password are case-sensitive (that is, "andyh" is not the same as "ANDYH", "Andyh" or "AndyH"). User name and password are usually both lower-case.

If you enter your password every time you connect, check that you haven't hit the Caps Lock key by accident - it's surprisingly easy to do this.

CHAPTER THREE

The World-Wide Web

The World-Wide Web is one of the most immediate and easy-to-use services on the Internet. This chapter explains how to use a browser - the program you use to access Web pages - and looks at some of the interesting places to go to.

Covers

Introduction

The World-Wide Web (WWW) is one of the most immediate, and easy-to-use, services on the Internet. The Web is made up of a series of "pages", containing both formatted text and in-line graphics. These pages can contain links to other pages (which can be anywhere else on the Internet), and can also have things like radio buttons, pull-down menus and fill-in boxes which allow you to enter information. To select these links, just click on them with the mouse.

You view WWW documents using a program called a "browser". There are a number of these available: in this book I'll concentrate on Netscape Navigator, which is one of the most popular. Netscape also allows you to read and send eMail and to access Usenet news, but these services are covered in later chapters.

The main competition to Netscape is Microsoft Internet Explorer. The main advantage of this application is that Microsoft give it away for free; individuals can register Netscape for free "for evaluation", but it is a commercial software package, and should really be paid for. If you want a registered copy of Netscape, which allows you support from the manufacturers and a printed manual, it is available for $35 - about £20.

REMEMBER

You need to be dialled in for the whole time that you are using a WWW browser - you can end up with quite a big phone bill if you use the Web too much!

There are things which Netscape can do which Internet Explorer can't, and vice versa, but in general they are about equally powerful, and it really doesn't matter which one you use. A lot of people keep copies of both of them on their computer, using whichever one is best for a particular site.

To run a browser, you must first be connected to the Internet, either by a permanent connection, or by a dial-up connection using an Internet provider. See Chapter Two for details of how to do this.

Web Browsers

The two major Web browsers, Netscape and Internet Explorer, are much of a muchness: the way the World-Wide Web is designed means that any browser must fulfil many standard criteria if it is to be used to access all (or most of) the pages that are out there. Thus, while the screenshots on the following pages are taken from Netscape, users of Internet Explorer should see something very similar.

This is what you see when you run Netscape:

These button bars allow you to navigate between pages, and point you to interesting places.

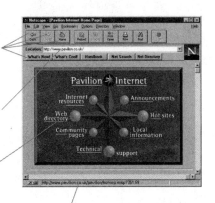

This box shows the location of the current page.

The first page that loads when your browser is started is known as your "Home Page" - in my case, it's that of Pavilion Internet, my service provider.

If you point to a link with your mouse, this box will show you where it leads to.

Links to other places ("hotlinks") are underlined. Links which you have visited before are in red: those which you have not visited are in blue. It is possible to use images for links: these are outlined in red or blue. There are also what are called "image maps": these allow the author of a page to specify hotlinks on an image (for example, on the page above, you can click on the points of the star to go to different places).

World-Wide Web Addresses

Every page on the World-Wide Web has its own individual address, which tells your Web browser where to find it. This address is called a URL, short for Uniform Resource Locator. A URL looks like this:

HANDY TIP

If you already know the URL of a site, you can just type it into the location box, and the browser will go there.

`http://www.pavilion.co.uk/westdean/House.jpg`

The "service type". This identifies a URL and tells Netscape what to do with it.

The Internet address on which the item is found. This is an Internet Domain Name.

The location on the remote site where the item is found. This file is an image file in "JPEG" format, which is why it ends with ".jpg".

Service Types

The first part of a URL identifies the type of service it points to. Most URLs start with "http://", which means that they are ordinary WWW addresses (the "http" stands for "Hypertext Transfer Protocol", which is the system Netscape uses to fetch WWW pages). There is an older and simpler service that you may find, called "Gopher". You may encounter Gopher sites if you look at University information systems; Internet Explorer and Netscape are quite happy to handle them. The URL of a Gopher site will begin with "gopher://". It's also possible to use your Web browser to access anonymous FTP sites (see Chapter Six), in which case the URL will begin with "ftp://". There are a couple of other service types - especially Usenet news ("news:"), or eMail ("mailto:").

Domain Names

Every site on the Internet, whether accessed by WWW, eMail, FTP etc., is addressed by its Internet "domain name".

A domain name is composed a bit like an address on an envelope: just as on an envelope you start with your house number, then your street, then the town, then the county, in an Internet Domain name you have a series of "domains", getting more general as we go from right to left. In the URL we've looked at, the domain name is:

www.pavilion.co.uk

Taking things from right to left, the ".uk" shows that the site is in the UK. A site in France ends with ".fr"; a site in Japan ends with ".jp". An Australian site uses ".au" or sometimes, for historical reasons ".oz"; a site in Croatia (yes, there are a few) ends in ".hr". Don't ask me what "hr" stands for, though. Some domain names don't end with a country code: these are usually (but not always) in the USA. There is a ".us" domain, but it's not often used - the Americans don't put their country on their domains for a similar reason to why we don't put the country on our stamps - they were there first.

The next domain to the left is ".co", which indicates a commercial organisation. A similar US site would use ".com". An academic organisation such as a university would use ".ac" (or in the US, ".edu"). There are a few other domain designations: the Government use either ".gov" or ".govt" (they can't seem to make up their minds), there is a ".sch" domain for the schools who are beginning to appear on the net: Non-profit organisations use ".org", and backbone Internet organisations use ".net" - hence the name of the magazine.

The ".pavilion" indicates that this site is at Pavilion Internet, my Internet provider. Anything to the left of that part is up to the organisation to assign: in this case we have "www", which designates the machine Pavilion have which handles the World-Wide Web.

Navigating With Your Browser

When you view a Web page using your browser, you will see hotlinks on the page. These are underlined, like this:

 HANDY TIP

If you click and hold on a hotlink, a menu will pop up allowing you to save the link to disk, etc.

To follow the hotlink, click on it with the mouse.

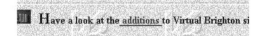

 REMEMBER

A link you've visited before will be displayed in a different colour (usually red rather than blue).

You can always retrace your steps or go back to your home page by clicking on the appropriate buttons.

The browser keeps track of the pages you've visited in your current session. At any time you can go back to an earlier page by using the "Go..." menu.

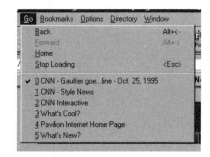

The Bookmark List

Any time you encounter a WWW page that you might want to look at again, you can put it on your bookmark list. Netscape will remember this list between sessions.

Internet Explorer uses a similar method of storing the URLs of your favourite Web pages: click on "Add to Favorites" from the Favorites menu.

Select "Add Bookmark" from the Bookmark menu to add the current page to your bookmark list.

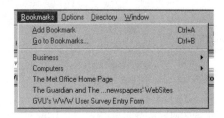

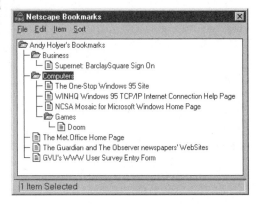

Netscape's "Bookmarks" window allows you to drag elements in your bookmark list around, and insert headers and separators.

If you select an element in the Bookmark window and choose "Properties" from the "Item" menu, you get this window which allows you to rename the bookmark and add notes.

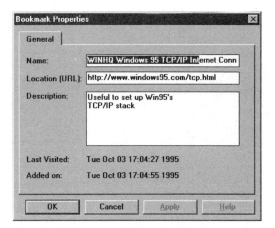

Exchanging Bookmark Lists

Netscape keeps your bookmark list as a file on your hard disk called "BOOKMARK.HTM". This can be read directly by Netscape or another WWW browser, so you can send your bookmark list to a friend, by putting it on a floppy disk, or attaching it to an eMail.

HANDY TIP

Similarly, you can exchange Internet Explorer's Favorites: they're located in the C:\Windows\Favorites folder on your hard drive.

Netscape will import any .htm file, extract the hotlinks, and put it in your bookmark list. This means that not only can you take someone else's BOOKMARK.HTM file, but you can take any list of WWW sites you may find and put it on your bookmark list. Select Import from the file menu of Netscape's Bookmark list.

If you find a list of links which you are interested in while browsing the Internet, you can save the page as a .htm file by using the "Save as" option from Netscape.

Interesting Sites

The Internet is growing all the time: over 100 new World-Wide Web sites are added every day. In the next few pages, I'll point you at a few sites which may be of interest. In each heading is the site's URL: type this into your Web browser's location box to go to this site.

SCIENCE

The Met. Office
http://www.meto.govt.uk/

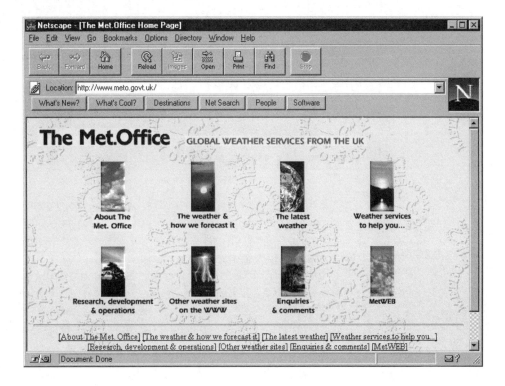

This site carries information on the work of the Met Office, each day's weather forecast, satellite images of the UK, and pointers to other weather-based sites.

NASA
http://www.nasa.gov/

This site has links to more or less every space-related resource that you would ever want to see. There is day-by-day news of shuttle missions (during missions, you even get up-to-the-minute details of the progress of the mission). There is a library of photographs and movies which NASA have access to, news and pictures of the Hubble Space Telescope, and (for science teachers) useful suggestions for lessons and teaching resources.

When I was six, I really wanted to go to the moon. This is about as close as I'm likely to get.

MEDIA

The Electronic Telegraph
http://www.telegraph.co.uk/

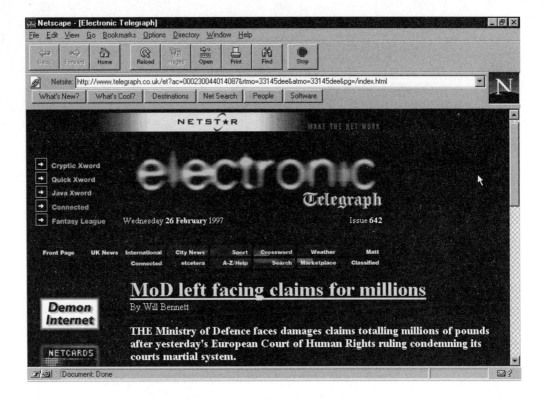

By choice, I read the Guardian, but there's no denying that the Daily Telegraph provides one of the best on-line news services in the UK.

The Electronic Telegraph is published at 7:30 am every weekday, and carries an abbreviated version of that day's paper. From comparing it with the printed copy, about 40% of the day's paper is included (including the cartoons and the crossword).

To get beyond the headlines, you need to register on-line to get a username and password. This is free - the Telegraph supports the service through advertising, and they need to show their advertisers who reads it.

Time Out
http://www.timeout.co.uk/

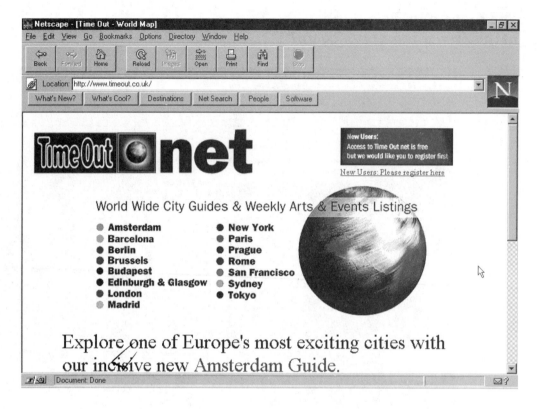

Time Out provide a weekly listings service not just for London, but also for a range of other cities around the world. New cities are being added all the time.

I have used the service myself (printing out the events pages the day before leaving to go on holiday), and it really is as useful as the printed magazine.

This is another site with which you need to register.

The BBC
http://www.bbc.co.uk/

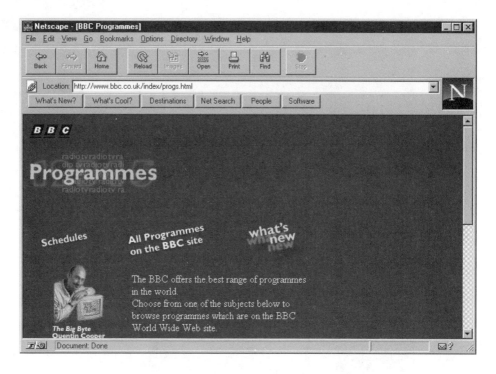

The BBC's server, it has to be said, leaves something to be desired. Some programmes have extensive coverage (those connected with computers, for example), while other areas have minimal information and even the occasional out-of-date listings page.

The BBC have invested some resources into sorting this out, and hopefully it will have some effect in the future.

Private Eye
http://www.intervid.co.uk/eye

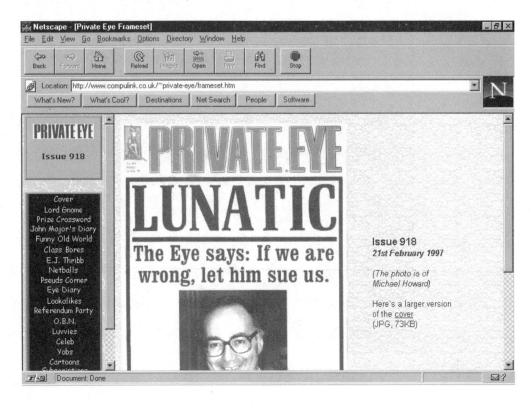

Of less use for regular readers of The Eye than for those who read it occasionally. This server carries most of the regular features and a selection of cartoons from the latest edition.

There are net-specific versions of some of the regular features - for example the "Netballs" entries don't appear in the printed "Colemanballs" column.

In keeping with the printed edition's obsession with carrying ads begging you to subscribe, yes, you can subscribe to the printed version from the Web page.

POLITICS

HM Government
http://www.open.gov.uk/

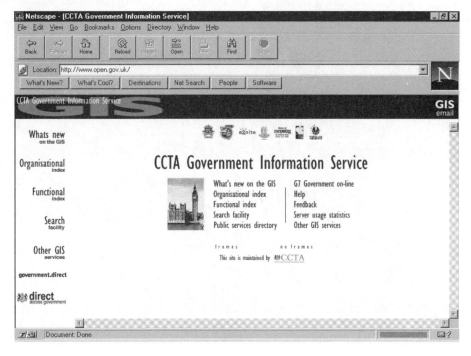

This service provides official information servers for a range of government departments and for some government organisations.

The quality of different departments' services can be rather variable: for some it amounts to little more than a press release.

One surprising service is HM Treasury's service: they publish every press release produced by the Treasury in the past two years, along with transcripts of speeches and minutes of monthly meetings with the Bank of England. It's quite interesting to see the announcements which go to the newspapers in their original form as they arrive. This service is also quite interesting on Budget day.

The other service of real use is the Stationery Office, which posts a daily transcript of Hansard on its pages.

The White House
http://www.whitehouse.gov/

This is one of those pages which everyone looks at when they're first on the Internet. In particular, if you follow the link for "The First Family" you get to a little photo essay which among other things includes a picture, and sound sample, of Socks the cat. This usually gets a laugh first time round. After that, forget it.

On a more useful note, this is the first port of call for a wide range of US Government services including the CIA, FBI and the Smithsonian Institute.

A useful thing the CIA server provides is its "World Fact Book". This is distributed to US embassies etc., and every year when they publish a new edition they put the old version on the Internet. It lists every country in the world and gives a useful set of statistics for each.

SEARCH ENGINES

Yahoo
http://www.yahoo.co.uk/

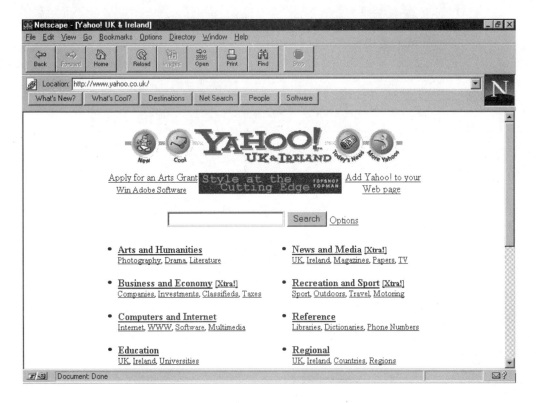

There are a number of sites on the Internet which act as a sort of directory service. Of these Yahoo is my favourite. Yahoo has links to thousands and thousands of URLs, ranging from individual home pages up to large corporations. It allows you to search by category or to use keywords to run a computerised search.

If you're looking for information on a particular topic, Yahoo is one of the best places to start. In addition, Yahoo keeps a list of its most popular links, and allows to you go to an entirely random location, if you so wish.

Yahoo has local sites all around the world. Besides providing faster access, they carry local content. This is the UK and Ireland version.

AltaVista
http://www.altavista.digital.com/

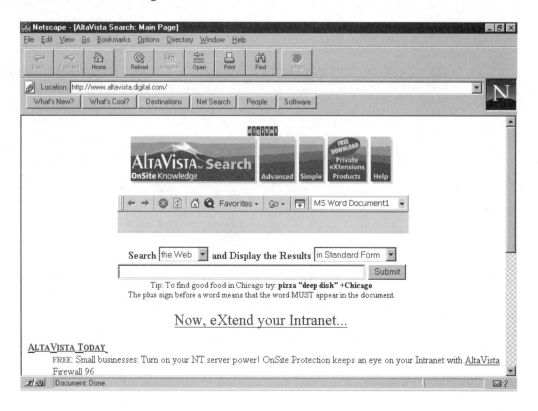

AltaVista is a product of the Digital Equipment Corporation. If you're very old you might have heard of their VAX or PDP-11 mini-computers: nowadays, their leading product is a server computer called an Alpha, and AltaVista is a demonstration of how impressive the hardware and software of the Alpha is. When you try it, you'll see what a good advert it is.

AltaVista is distinctive for how quickly it responds, and for quite how many sites it has indexed. AltaVista runs "robot" programs which go out over the Internet, pulling in pages and then indexing them. This means that even obscure pages can turn up: I've found pages using AltaVista which I wrote myself and have since forgotten about.

It's quite a fun game (as long as your name isn't "Smith") to put your name into AltaVista and see what it comes up with. I've found a distant cousin this way.

Excite
http://www.excite.com/

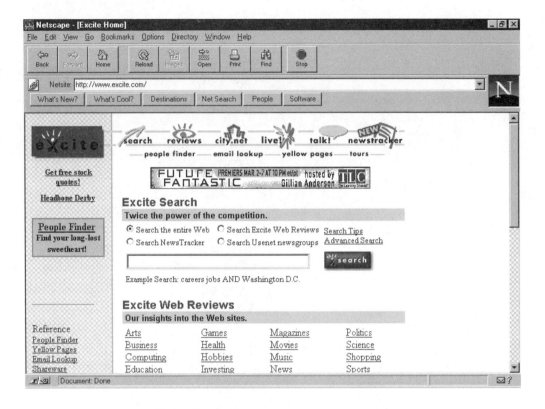

Excite is another index site, which tries to be a bit like a cross between Yahoo and AltaVista. Since it's a more recent site, the result is a lot more glossy.

Besides the search and catalogue functions, Excite carries a number of other services, including finding shareware, maps, and local information. Most of this information is US-specific, but it is still fascinating, especially when you should be looking for something else entirely.

Excite's best feature is the quality of its search. It seems almost magically to come up with exactly what you wanted, and you can ask almost natural-language questions.

The Internet Bookshop
http://www.bookshop.co.uk/

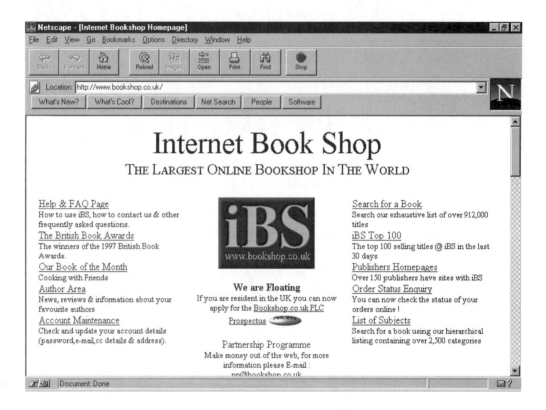

Commercial sites on the Internet are often a disappointment - many of them are little more than an advert. The Internet Bookshop is one of the few sites from which you might actually want to buy something.

The Internet Bookshop provides a range of books you would expect from a normal bookshop. In addition it allows you to do searches by Publisher, Author and Title.

To buy something from the Bookshop, you need to supply them with a credit card number (by telephone or fax) and they will then debit your card every time you order.

Oh, and have a look at:

`http://www.bookshop.co.uk/ComputerStep/`

Barclay Square
http://www.itl.net/barclaysquare/

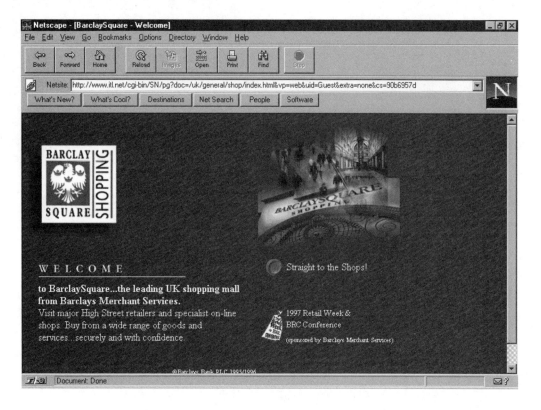

A recent development on the Internet is the appearance of "on-line shopping malls". The biggest problem with most of these is that since they're based in the USA, there's nothing for us to buy. This site, run by Barclays Bank is firmly aimed at the UK.

Besides information on Barclays and Barclaycard, you can visit Toys R Us, Argos and Innovations. For a change, you can actually buy things here - though I have to say that I haven't been tempted yet.

Computer Step
http://www.computerstep.com/

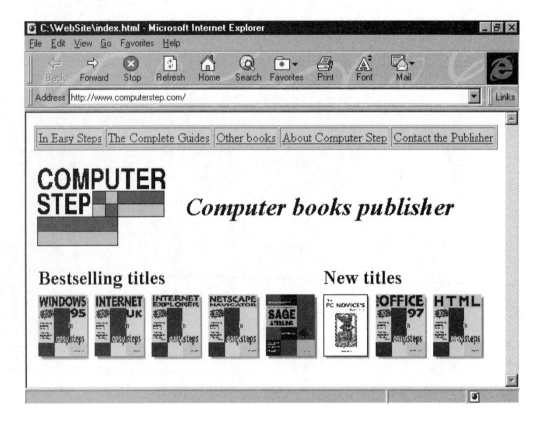

Well, we have to show our own Web site, don't we? On this site you can find up-to-date details on all of Computer Step's publications, including the "in easy steps" books, and the "Complete Guide" range. You'll see an image of each book's cover, and a complete contents listing.

If you have any questions or comments regarding the Web site or any of Computer Step's books, there's a hotlink which you can use to send eMail to the Publisher.

Cerberus Sound+Vision
http://www.cdj.co.uk/

You can't (yet) connect to The Virgin Megastore to buy CDs on-line (though there are a couple of U.S. sites which offer this service). Cerberus' Digital Jukebox offers the next best thing.

You register with Cerberus, giving them your credit card number, and you receive in return a Windows application to install on your PC. From then on, for a few pence a time, you can download any of a wide range of songs. These aren't just clips - they're the full versions of songs (sometimes unreleased versions), in CD-quality stereo. Plug a tape recorder into your sound card, and you've got a single nobody else has got. There are some quite big record labels and artists there, too.

Customising Your Browser

One of the odd things about the World-Wide Web is that the appearance of a page is largely under the control of the browser, rather than that of the writer of the page. You can change the fonts which your browser uses to display pages, and the default background and text colours. If you want to view pages in Old English text, in green on white, then you can. More seriously, I find this quite useful: I'm short-sighted, and late in the day it's nice to be able to increase the font size to ease my eyes.

 To change the fonts in Internet Explorer, select "Options" from the View menu and choose the "General" tab, then click on the "Font Settings" button.

 Besides English (or "Latin1") text, Netscape can also handle Japanese and Eastern European encodings. Select the one you want.

1 Select "General" from the "Options" menu.

2 Select the "Fonts" tab.

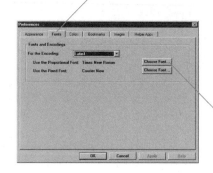

3 For each encoding, Netscape allows you to define a fixed and a variable-width font. Click on "Choose Font".

4 Select the font and size you require.

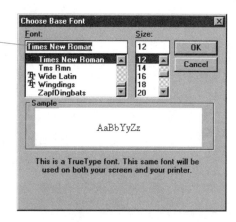

Helper Applications

Besides text and images, there are a wide variety of types of data to be found on the World-Wide Web. Amongst the most showy are video and sound. When it encounters a type of data which it cannot handle, your Web browser launches what is known as a "helper application". You can set up your browser to assign applications to different data types - you can use any application which you have on your machine. For example, if you have a good sound program (say, provided with your sound card), you can set your browser to use this for sounds. There exists a wide variety of useful tools for free on the Internet - often if you find a site with a novel type of data, there is a link to the appropriate helper.

As an example, here is how to set up Netscape to use Microsoft Word to read .rtf (Rich-Text Format) files:

HANDY TIP

Netscape and Internet Explorer use a system called "MIME" to identify data types. You can select data types by MIME category, by description, or by file type.

1 Select "General" from the "Options" menu. Choose the "Helper Apps" dialogue.

2 Select the data type for which you wish to assign a helper.

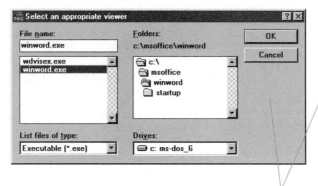

3 Select "Browse" to choose an application.

Plug-ins

The next stage up from a helper application is a Plug-in. This is a small program which you install in your browser, allowing the browser to handle new or unusual types of data. A helper application runs in its own window on your computer, whereas a Plug-in uses your browser window to display data - it's just as if your browser has suddenly acquired the ability to display the new type of data.

Companies often write a Plug-in which will handle the data produced by applications they produce. The Plug-in is available for anyone to download from the Internet, while anyone who wants to put that sort of data on their Web pages needs to buy the software to produce it.

The two best-known Plug-ins are Macromedia Shockwave and Real Player. Shockwave allows you to view files generated using Macromedia Director, a multimedia package. This allows much more interesting interaction than from a normal Web page. You can get Shockwave from Macromedia's Web site, **http://www.macromedia.com**.

The Real Player from Progressive Networks allows you to see and hear video and sound from a Real Audio or Real Video server. Normally you would need to download the whole of a video or sound file before you could see or hear it. The Real Player opens a special Internet connection so that you can see or hear the data as it arrives. There are even sites where you can listen to a radio station (for example) as it broadcasts - an example of this is Virgin Radio's site,

http://www.virginradio.com

You can download the Real Player from Progressive Networks' Web site,

http://www.real.com

There are commercial versions of the software which allow you to hear CD quality sound over the Internet, if you have a fast enough connection.

Active Content

There are a number of techniques that Web site designers use to put more elaborate content on Web pages. The first of these is Java. This is a programming language which is designed to work over the Internet. Java programs are called "Applets" and are designed such that if your browser needs to run an applet which it does not already have, it will automatically download it over the Internet. Java has great potential - the new "Network Computers" will only run Java - but so far it is mostly used to produce scrolling headlines and buttons which change colour when you point to them.

There is a variant of Java called JavaScript, in which the program code is written into the Web page itself, rather than being in a compiled file. This is a lot less powerful than Java, but as far as you are concerned it does the same sort of thing.

The third form of active content is Microsoft's ActiveX. This is based on OLE, which is the system Microsoft developed to allow you to link part of one program into another (e.g., to insert an Excel spreadsheet into a Word document). In its Internet form, this allows parts of documents, or more usually Visual Basic or Visual C++ programs, to appear as part of a Web site. An ActiveX program is referred to as a "Component". If you download a Web page which needs a component which you do not have, the browser will fetch it automatically.

Only Microsoft Internet Explorer can handle ActiveX directly. If you want to view ActiveX in Netscape, there is a Plug-in which will handle it for you.

You should take care with any type of active content. There are security features in all of these systems which should stop a nefarious program being run on your computer, but there have been viruses of one type or another passed around using all of them in the past few years. If you are worried about the consequences of this, you can turn off Java, JavaScript or ActiveX from your browser's Preferences dialogue box.

Caches and Proxies

There are a number of ways to make access to the World-Wide Web (at least appear) faster than it would be otherwise. The first of these is to set up a cache on your hard disk.

Setting up a Cache

You can set up your browser to use a set amount of your memory and disk space to store pages and images as it receives them over the Internet. The next time you try and load that page, the browser checks whether the page has changed: if it hasn't changed, then the browser uses the copy it has in the cache, and doesn't bother transferring the file over the Internet. A large (full-screen) image could take ten minutes to transfer: it only takes a second or so to get it from disk - and is instant from memory. Memory cache is cleared when you leave your browser, but disk cache will stay until the cache is full, or you intentionally clear the cache.

If you've got enough spare disk space to assign 20 Megabytes or more to cache, it will make pages you visit often appear to load far faster than they would otherwise.

HANDY TIP

To access the cache settings in Internet Explorer, select "Options" from the View menu, choose the "Advanced" tab, then click the "Settings" button.

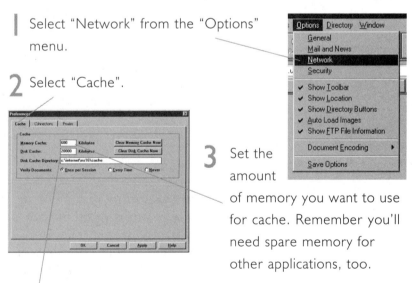

1 Select "Network" from the "Options" menu.

2 Select "Cache".

3 Set the amount of memory you want to use for cache. Remember you'll need spare memory for other applications, too.

4 Set the amount of disk you want to use as cache. If you can spare 20-30 Mb, it can make a lot of difference.

Proxies

Your Internet provider may provide a proxy service for the World-Wide Web. This is a system which is part of their WWW service, which (amongst other things) has a large amount of spare disk space.

To access Internet Explorer's proxy settings, select "Options" from the View menu, choose the "Connection" tab, and click on the "Settings" button.

When you request a WWW page, your Web browser contacts the proxy server. The proxy server checks to see if it has a copy of the page you have requested, and contacts the final site to see if its copy is up to date.

If the proxy has a new copy of the file, then it just sends it to you (which will be faster than you would receive it from the remote site). If it doesn't have a copy, or if its copy is out of date, it fetches a copy, puts it in its cache, and also sends it to you. Then if someone else requests the same page, it's delivered directly from the proxy.

Proxies are set up from the Network dialogue, just like cache.

1 Select Proxies.

2 Your provider can tell you if they provide a proxy service, and if so, which services they provide. Fill in the address and port number for each proxy.

3 Proxies can cause problems with some WWW pages - especially fill-in forms. If you have a problem with a particular page, put its address in this box.

Your Own World-Wide Web Page

After you have been using the World-Wide Web for a few months, the time will come when you'd like to contribute for yourself.

Besides the established sites I have described in this chapter, there are thousands of individual "Home Pages" set up by ordinary Internet users. These cover everything from pictures of their pets, through personal interests (a friend of mine runs quite a fun site about children's TV presenter Phillipa Forester), and a wide range of other interests.

World-Wide Web pages look very difficult to produce, but they are a lot easier than you'd think. In this book, I will give you a brief overview to get you started. For more information, read the book, "HTML in easy steps". There is a lot more information available on the WWW itself, which you should look at if you are interested.

HTTP Servers

An http server is the program which a Web browser contacts, and which sends out the pages when requested. To put up a WWW page, you need access to a server.

There are a wide range of servers available, including one which runs under Windows; however running your home page on your computer is not a good idea, since it would only be available when you were dialled in (it is in theory possible to leave yourself connected permanently, but besides the cost, providers tend to take a dim view of this).

The best answer is to get space on an existing WWW server. There are several ways to go about this. Firstly, some providers give you a small amount of space with your subscription; secondly, you may be lucky enough to "borrow" some space at a university or a large company. Finally, there are commercial services which will rent space on their servers (there are even one or two which provide a small amount free to individuals). You should prepare your pages on your own computer, and FTP them onto the host machine when they are ready.

See Chapter Six for details of how to do FTP.

HTML

World-Wide Web pages are written in Hypertext Mark-up Language, or HTML for short. Most of an HTML document is text, with "tags" marking the text to indicate changes of font, images etc.

This World-Wide Web page...

...looks like this in HTML.

Until recently, HTML was "a programming language you could learn in an afternoon". Since browser manufacturers have added their own tags, this is no longer true, but it is still very simple to learn.

Preparing your Pages

There are several ways to go about producing HTML. The simplest is to write it directly using WordPad (that's what I do), but this is obviously difficult if you're not used to programming. There exists a wide range of tools which allow you to generate HTML in a Windows environment. Microsoft Office 97 and a number of other packages can handle HTML documents.

HANDY TIP

Your Web browser will run happily without being dialled in. If you are using Windows 3.1 or 3.11, however, you may get the message "Unable to find WINSOCK.DLL". To solve this, run Trumpet, but *don't dial in.*

In any case, you already have the best tool available to try out your pages - your Web browser. By using the "Open File" option, you can view documents on your hard disk, and tweak them until they look right.

Images

You will probably want to include images in your pages. These files should be in GIF or JPEG format - most graphics packages can produce these. Avoid making the images too big - if you've got a 100K image on your page not many people will bother to look at it. A useful tip for GIF images is that as soon as the number of colours goes over a power of 2, the size of the file doubles - that is, a 17-colour GIF is twice the size of a 16-colour one.

Most browsers now handle JPEG images. These are much smaller than GIFs, but they do lose some detail (photographs actually look better, though). If you can put up with the loss, they're worth trying.

If you get pictures scanned, they'll usually come back scanned at 300 dots per inch - the resolution of a laser printer. For a WWW page you don't need this: most PC screens are between 70 and 100dpi. You get a better result if you scan at this resolution.

Tips

One nice thing about HTML is that it's an interpreted language - so when you load a page into your Web browser, you've got the HTML that produced it. You can either look at the HTML by using "View by Source" or save the file to your disk.

The best way to come up with your first WWW page is this:

1 Prepare any images that you may want to use. It's *not* considered polite to steal other people's pictures without asking, by the way.

2 Find a home page whose layout you like.

3 Save the page to disk as a .htm file.

4 Use the file as a template for your own page.

Forms, scripts, image maps etc.

You'll often come across sophisticated functions on WWW pages, which you would like to put on your own page.

These features need a degree of programming skill, and are far beyond the scope of this book. They are covered in depth in the book "HTML in easy steps", published by Computer Step.

Set Task: Searching by Subject

There are a number of catalogues and search tools on the Internet: try several to be sure you haven't missed anything.

This section shows you how to use Yahoo to find information on a particular subject. For the sake of argument let's do a search on "botany". I presume that you've already dialled in to your provider, run your Web browser, etc.

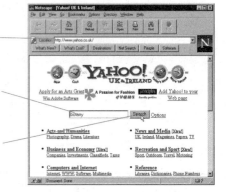

1 Point your browser at http://www.yahoo.co.uk/

2 Type "botany" in the box.

3 Click the "Search" button.

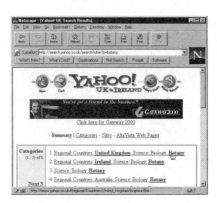

4 Yahoo displays a list of entries which have the word "botany" in the title.

5 Go to any links which look interesting by clicking on them.

Tips

Choose your search term carefully - a word like "car" will come up with lots of false matches. If you can, use more than one word.

You can save this page to disk if you want to keep it for later.

Remember that Yahoo has no control over links which are not on its site, so you may find that not all links work, and some may be very slow.

CHAPTER FOUR

Electronic Mail

Electronic Mail allows you to send personal messages to other people on the Internet. This chapter explains the principles of eMail, and looks into how to operate Eudora, one of the best eMail programs.

Covers

Introduction: Why Use eMail?

Electronic Mail (eMail for short) is one of the most basic services on the Internet. It will probably end up being one of the services you use the most - indeed, many Internet users never use any other service.

Electronic mail allows you to send text messages to one or more people on the Internet. These people do not need to be connected at the time that you send the message; their Internet provider will keep the messages until the next time they check their mail.

An eMail normally takes at most a few minutes to deliver anywhere in the world, so it is much faster than sending a letter (some parts of the world, for example Africa, are not yet directly connected to the Internet; in this case an eMail usually takes between a few hours and a few days to deliver - still faster than a letter). Many eMail programs allow you to attach files to an eMail, so that you can send someone a word processor document, a spreadsheet or even a program file.

The biggest problem if you wish to use eMail is that a lot of the people to whom you would send a letter or a fax do not yet have an eMail address. This state of affairs is beginning to change - you can now use eMail to send a letter to The Times, or a request to Radio One - but will be something to consider for a few years yet. For the last five years I've been wishing I could send eMail to my bank manager, but I still need to print the letter out and put it in an envelope, or fax it. Never mind, one day...

As it is, there are still plenty of people to talk to. There are a large number of "mailing lists" - lists of addresses to which you can add your name, and when anyone sends a message to the list, everyone on the list gets it. There are lists on anything from rock music to mobile phones, and they are all free to subscribe to. The only problem is that each list adds to the number of mail messages you receive each day.

Eudora: the eMail Program

As usual, there are a number of different programs that you can use to send and receive eMail. The one I will look at is Eudora, which is agreed to be one of the best.

 HANDY TIP

To use Eudora, your mail must be stored on a system which runs the "POP" protocol. Ask your Internet provider if they provide this service.

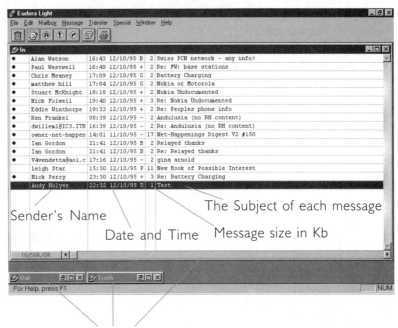

Sender's Name

Date and Time

The Subject of each message

Message size in Kb

These are three Eudora mailboxes. The "In" box is open: it is where your mail is stored. The "Out" box is where messages go while waiting to be sent, and the "Trash" box is where deleted mail is kept until it is emptied.

There are two versions of Eudora available: "Eudora Lite", which is available as Freeware, and a full-scale commercial version. The full version has a number of useful features (in particular, you can get Eudora to sort your mail by category before you read it), and also comes with a printed manual and one year's telephone support. The full version costs $65, less if you buy a number of copies at once, say for a company. Eudora Lite is a completely usable system, however: many people never upgrade.

Sending an eMail

To send a new eMail, select "New Message" from Eudora's "Message.." menu:

 HANDY TIP

To open the message sending window quickly, press Control-N.

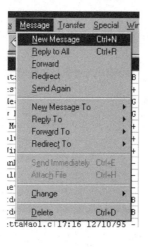

Eudora will then open a new message window:

 HANDY TIP

Put your regular contacts' eMail addresses on your Nickname list.

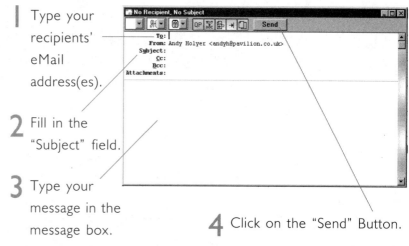

1 Type your recipients' eMail address(es).

2 Fill in the "Subject" field.

 HANDY TIP

You can paste all or part of your message from another application: however, all formatting (bold, italic etc.) will be removed.

3 Type your message in the message box.

4 Click on the "Send" Button.

Other Headers

If you want to send copies of the message to someone else, put their eMail address in the "Cc:" field (it stands for "Carbon copy").

If you want to send a copy to someone without anyone else knowing, put them in the "Bcc:" field (Blind carbon copy).

Replying to an eMail

If you have received an eMail, you can send a reply without having to type in the sender's eMail address and text. Select "Reply" from the "Messages" menu. You will see a window like this:

Eudora fills in the return address and Subject for you.

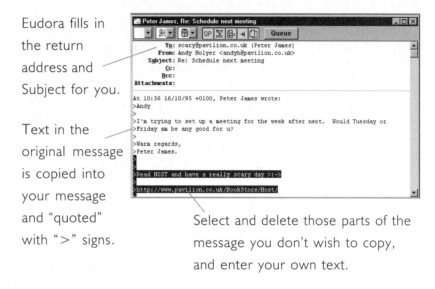

Text in the original message is copied into your message and "quoted" with ">" signs.

Select and delete those parts of the message you don't wish to copy, and enter your own text.

Be very careful to check all the return addresses Eudora fills in for you - if the mail was addressed to more than one person, you'll reply to all of them, which may not be what you want.

Trim the quoted text as much as possible - it's considered very bad manners to quote someone's entire mail message just to add a one-line reply.

Other Tips

The only time that you *must* be connected to your Internet provider is when you click on the Send button. You can take all the time that you want to compose your messages, and only connect when you wish to send them. See "Working Off-line" for more details.

You may put as many eMail addresses as you like in the To: Cc: and Bcc: fields. Simply separate the addresses with a comma. Only one copy of the message will be sent by Eudora to your provider: their software will do all the work of sending different copies to different places.

eMail Addresses

All Internet eMail addresses look like this:

name@machine.name

Usually, the person's account name on their system

The domain name of their Internet connection

For example, my eMail address is:

andyh@pavilion.co.uk

My account name is "andyh"

My provider is Pavilion Internet in Brighton: their domain name is pavilion.co.uk

See the section "Domain Names", in Chapter Three, for a longer explanation of how domain names work.

Finding Someone's eMail Address

If you want to send someone an eMail but don't know their address, you have to do a little work. There is no complete "Phone Book" of people's eMail addresses. There are a couple of on-line services which claim to act as eMail phone books, but these are less than comprehensive.

The simplest thing to do is to ask them. Fortunately, more and more people are putting their eMail addresses on business cards and letter headings.

If you know where they work, you can often guess what their eMail address would be. For instance, suppose you want to send a message to John Jones who works for the BBC. The BBC's domain name is "bbc.co.uk". It's worth trying to send a trial message to: "J.Jones@bbc.co.uk".

All Internet sites which receive eMail have a person whose responsibility is to sort out problems with mail. They set up a special eMail address for this purpose, called "postmaster". If you know that the person you want to mail has an account on a particular service, then sending a (polite!) eMail to the Postmaster at that site is often effective. For example if you have a friend who you know uses Demon Internet, then an eMail to "postmaster@demon.co.uk" should be able to find the answer.

BEWARE **Don't worry: if the address you try belongs to nobody, you'll just get your message returned. However, it is possible to accidentally send a message to the wrong person, so don't be too personal!**

Odd Cases

There are a couple of cases where you have to play around with someone's eMail address in order to send them a message from the Internet. The most common of these is if they have an account with CompuServe. CompuServe accounts consist of two numbers with a comma between them, for example "12345,9876". The trick is this: change the comma to a ".", and add "@compuserve.com" on the end. In this case, address your mail to "12345.9876@compuserve.com".

Signature Files

You'll find that it is very useful to be able to "sign" eMails, giving details about yourself which are not provided by the mail headers - your telephone or fax numbers, for example. It would be tedious to have to type out all this information every time you compose an eMail, so Eudora allows you to fill in a "Signature". This text will be attached to the end of every mail you send, unless you tell Eudora not to.

To set up a signature, select "Signature" from the Windows menu:

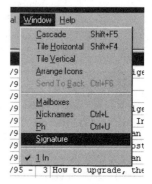

You will see a window like this appear: Enter the text that you would like in the window and close it.

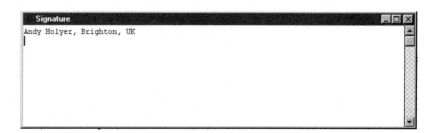

When you send a message, this button controls whether your signature file is included or not.

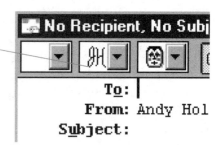

There are various fashions in the design of signature files. Some people put descriptions of what they do, their home address, adverts for mailing lists and/or WWW sites, quotes from favourite books films or pop songs, and even little cartoons made from keyboard characters. Some people have signatures which take up half a page or more.

While these can be fun for a while, remember that if someone gets a lot of mail messages from you, a signature, especially one that takes up a lot of space, is soon going to end up boring. As a rule of thumb, a signature should be as short as possible, and should *never* take up more than four lines. Using underlines to make up a box for the signature is also frowned on. It's a free Internet, but remember: signature files are rather like car stickers: the longer your signature, the lower you are held in esteem by many people on the Net.

Attaching Files

A drawback with eMail in general is that a message should normally only consist of ASCII text - that is, the characters you can see on your keyboard, with no bold, italic etc. and no foreign characters. This is because when an eMail is sent it is passed between several computers to get to its destination, and some of them may do funny things with any unusual characters it may contain.

This is tricky if you want to send someone a program, word processor file, image etc. Eudora (and most other modern mail programs) allow you to "attach" one or more files to a message. When the message is sent, Eudora packages the file up, so that it will be sent successfully. When Eudora receives a message with an attachment, it decodes the file, and places the file on your hard disk.

HANDY TIP

Eudora uses the MIME standard for attaching files, and a system called "ßinHex" (actually a Macintosh format) to encode binary data. Software to handle these formats for non PC/Mac platforms is available from most Internet software archives.

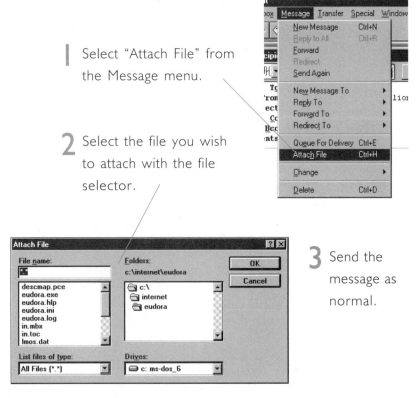

1 Select "Attach File" from the Message menu.

2 Select the file you wish to attach with the file selector.

3 Send the message as normal.

Nicknames

It can be tricky remembering people's eMail addresses, so Eudora allows you to keep a list of "Nicknames".

HANDY TIP

You can take an address from a message in your mailbox using the "Make Nickname" command.

I Select "Nicknames" from the "Windows" menu.

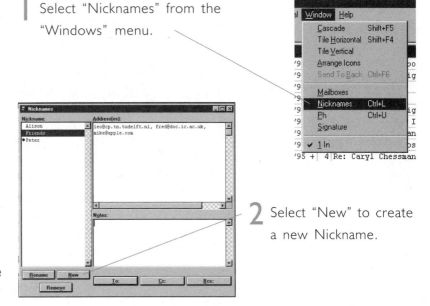

2 Select "New" to create a new Nickname.

REMEMBER

A Nickname can point to more than one eMail address: this is useful if you regularly send mail to a number of people at once - say a list of customers to whom you regularly send announcements.

3 Enter the Nickname you require. If you select this box, the name will be added to the "Message To..." pull-down menu.

Working Off-line

As delivered, Eudora assumes that you will be connected to the Internet all the time that you are running the program - if your company or organization is connected through a leased line or an ISDN link this will be the case. If you use a dial-up connection to a commercial Internet provider however, you will find that this is a waste of money. You only need to be connected when you are fetching or sending mail - the rest of the time you can disconnect and save on your phone bill. This is how to set Eudora to work like this:

If you make these modifications, you will need to deliberately check mail (use Control-M) and send mail (use Control-T). Eudora will no longer do this for you. However, Eudora will send any queued messages each time you do a check.

1 Select the Settings... option from the Special menu.

2 Select "Checking Mail" in the Category window.

3 Make sure that "Check mail every ... minutes" is set to "0".

4 Select "Sending Mail" in the Category window.

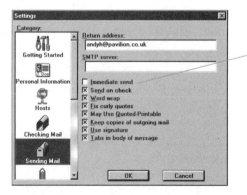

5 Make sure that the "Immediate send" check box is not set. You will now find that the sending mail panel has a "Queue" button rather than "Send".

CHAPTER FIVE

Usenet News

Usenet News is a worldwide bulletin-board system which allows you to take part in discussions on a wide range of topics. This chapter looks at the software you need to access news, and describes some interesting groups.

Covers

Introduction

Usenet News is the main public discussion space on the Internet. Despite its name, it carries very little actual "news", as in current events etc. Whereas eMail is generally one-to-one, News allows one-to-many communication.

News consists of a large number of "newsgroups" (at the last count there were over 12,000 of them). Each of them covers a different topic. Messages "posted" to a group are sent to a local "News Server", and are then passed from one server to another (a message takes about a day to go round the world). Messages can then be read by anyone who "subscribes" to that group.

Groups vary from serious technical discussion (a good way to get answers to technical problems) to just plain silly (but fun once in a while).

This chapter describes Free Agent, a popular program for reading news, describes how newsgroups are organised, and gives some pointers on how to get the most out of reading news.

Free Agent - a News Reader

There are a number of programs available which allow you to read and post news. Apart from Free Agent (described here), there are several other choices (for example, the new version of Netscape provides a full newsreader).

Free Agent is commercial software by Forte Inc. This is a free version of a similar product called just Agent - available for $29 ($40 if you want disks and a manual too).

Free Agent's big advantage over most of its rivals is that you can set it up to operate off-line - that is, you can connect, download all new messages in the groups you read, and then disconnect while you read them. This saves a lot of connect time (and thus phone bills).

This button bar allows you to control most of Agent's functions.

This is a list of newsgroups you have subscribed to.

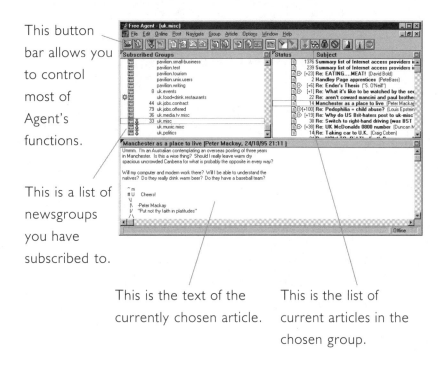

This is the text of the currently chosen article.

This is the list of current articles in the chosen group.

Configuring Free Agent

Before you can use Free Agent for the first time, you need to supply it with some information. Your Internet provider may have done this for you, but if not, select "Preferences" from the "Options" menu, and select "System Profile".

 HANDY TIP

Your provider can tell you the name of your news and mail servers if you don't know them.

1 Put the address of your local News Server in this box.

2 Put the address of your eMail server in this box.

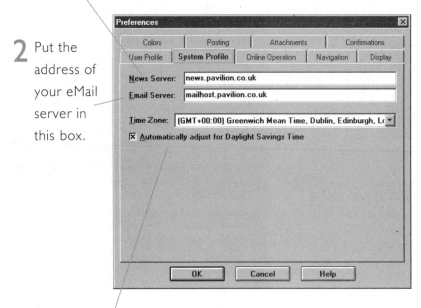

3 Select your time zone from the list (in the UK, this should be GMT as shown).

...contd

Next, select "User Profile":

1 Put your eMail address in this box (see Chapter Four).

2 Fill in your real name. You can put more-or-less anything in this box.

3 Put your organization (company name or college etc.) in this box.

Preferences				✕
Colors	Posting	Attachments		Confirmations
User Profile	System Profile	Online Operation	Navigation	Display

Email Address: `andyh@pavilion.co.uk`

Full Name: `Andy Holyer`

Organization: `                    `

Reply To: `                    `

┌─ News Server Authorization ─────────────────────┐
☐ Server requires authorization login

User Name: `                    `

☐ Remember Password between sessions

Password: `                    `
└───┘

[OK] [Cancel] [Help]

4 If you want replies to go to a different eMail address, put it in this box.

5 Very few News servers require an account name and password, but if your local one does, put them in these boxes. (Your provider can tell you if this is necessary and, if so, what to fill in.)

Your First News Session

The first time you run agent (or any other news reader) you need to download the full list of newsgroups on your local server. Since there are thousands of them, this can take a little while, so be prepared to go and make a cup of tea while they're arriving. Make sure you're dialled in to your local provider before you start this process.

1 Select "Refresh Groups List" from the On-line menu.

2 Ignore the radio button settings in the dialogue box - they are only of interest if you've already downloaded the groups list, and want to check you haven't missed anything.

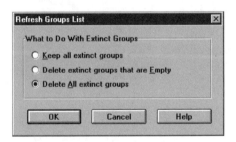

3 Select "OK".

4 Wait.

The length of time downloading the groups list depends on your modem speed and how many groups your provider carries, but between 5 and 20 minutes is about average. You can check that things are happening by looking at Agent's status display, or watching your modem's lights.

Once you've downloaded the list, you may as well disconnect, and go through the groups list and choose which groups you wish to subscribe to.

Subscribing to Groups

Next, you should subscribe to the groups which you wish to follow. This means that Agent will then check these groups for new articles. Don't worry about subscribing to too many groups - it's easy to unsubscribe.

I From the Group menu, select "Show All Groups".

2 Go through the list of groups, and choose the ones you'd like to subscribe to. I describe the different groups later in this chapter.

HANDY TIP

You can select a range of groups by holding down the shift key as you select them.

3 Select each group in turn.

4 Press the "subscribe" button. You'll see a little newspaper icon appear next to the group name.

BEWARE

Some groups have hundreds of postings per day: too many of these, and you could be spending an hour or so just getting the message subjects! A full news feed is over 300 Mb per day - you'll never read all of it.

5 To make it easier to see what you're doing, finally select "Show Only Subscribed Groups" from the Group menu.

When you subscribe to a group, the other subscribers have no way of knowing this; you are simply telling your browser what to ask for. Many people spend months just snooping on a group without posting anything: they're called "lurkers".

Your Daily News Regime

You can use Agent to read news in two ways. If you have a permanent connection to the Internet (or if you don't have to bother about keeping the phone bill down), you can set up Agent to operate in its on-line mode. This means that Agent is connected to the News server for the whole time you are reading news, collecting articles one at a time.

REMEMBER

The header of a news posting carries various information about the message, including its subject, the sender's name, and the size of the message.

For the rest of us, it's cheaper on the phone bill to set up Agent to operate off-line. This means that Agent will fetch new message headers, collect messages you wish to read, and send any responses you may have set up all in one go. You can then read news off-line, while you're not running up the phone bill (reading and replying to news is the most time-consuming part). The problem with this is that you need to be more disciplined in reading news: often you'll need to connect twice, once to get the headers, and then again to fetch the bodies of any messages you want to read.

Setting Agent for on-line or off-line operation

1 Select Preferences from the Options menu.

2 Select Online Operation.

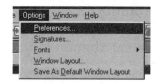

3 Select either Online Defaults or Offline Defaults depending on the mode you wish to use. This only sets the other options to the best for that mode: if you don't like a setting, then you can still change it later.

In the following sections, I'll assume that you're operating off-line, since on-line is very similar, but simpler.

Fetching New Article Headers

1 Use Trumpet to connect yourself to your Internet Provider.

2 Click on the "Get New Headers in Subscribed Groups" button.

HANDY TIP

While you're waiting for news to arrive, you can read mail or browse the World-Wide Web - but remember that the data coming from your modem will be divided between all the transfers going on at one time (so Agent will take longer to fetch the data).

3 Wait. If you're subscribed to a number of groups, it will take a while to fetch the headers. If you're reading a lot of high-traffic groups, it's worth allowing at least half an hour for Agent to finish.

4 When Agent is finished and has gone off-line, disconnect from your provider.

You are now in a position to choose which articles to fetch.

Selecting articles to download

1 Select each subscribed newsgroup in turn.

2 Select each article you wish to download.

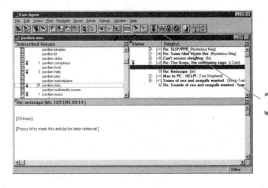

3 Double-click to mark it for downloading (or press the "download" button).

Finally

1 Reconnect to your provider.

2 Press the "Get Marked Article Bodies" button.

3 Wait (again).

Reading a Newsgroup

When you select a newsgroup from the list of all groups, you will see a list of messages currently in that group. What happens next depends on whether you're operating on-line or off-line. If you're off-line, the messages will be already fetched (assuming you've followed the instructions earlier). If you're on-line, you have to fetch each message as you look at it, which takes a few seconds.

A Newsgroup listing looks like this:

HANDY TIP

You can make the News- groups, Group or article window full-screen by typing "Z" (for "zoom") or by using the zoom button in the top right-hand corner.

Articles marked with ⤓ have not yet been fetched, but are marked to do so.

Articles marked with 🗋 have been fetched, and can be read now.

Articles marked with ⧫ [+2] are threads - see the next section.

A number in this column shows the number of lines in the message.

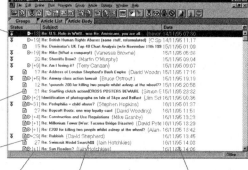

This is the title of each article (and the poster's name).

This is the date the article was posted.

To view the text of a message which has already been fetched, simply select it (if you've zoomed the group box, double-click the message).

To go on to the next message in a group, type "N" or press the 🔲 button.

To skip to the next thread, type "T" or press the 🔲 button.

To skip to the next newsgroup on your list, type "S" or press the 🔲 button.

Threads

A series of news postings following each other, one after another, is called a "thread". Agent will group articles in a thread together, regardless of other unconnected posts which may have arrived in between.

Agent shows a thread in the group list like this:

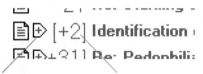

Click this symbol to "expand" the thread, to show its individual postings.	The "+2" shows that there are two follow-ups to this post - so there are three postings in the thread.

You can tell Agent to watch a thread by typing "W". Agent will then automatically collect new articles in that thread when it encounters them in future downloads.

Conversely, you can tell Agent to ignore a thread by typing "I". Agent will mark the whole thread read, and will never collect a message in this thread again. This can cut down your on-line time quite a bit, after a while.

Postings and Follow-ups

A completely new news message is called a *posting*; if you reply to someone else's posting, it's called a *follow-up*.

You can follow-up to newsgroups, by eMail to individuals, or both at once.

| To make a posting, press one of these buttons:

Post new news message.

Follow-up to current news message.

Send eMail.

Reply to current message by eMail.

2 Check the headers to see that they're correct (see below).

3 (if following up) Trim the quoted text to as small as is still meaningful.

4 Enter your text.

5 If you're on-line at the time, press "Send Now". If not, press "Send Later" - it'll be sent the next time Agent connects to the news server.

Posting: Header Fields

The headers of a News posting are very important, and can get quite involved, so it's worth going through the more important ones.

 In a follow-up, check the groups listed very carefully. It's considered bad manners to follow up to inappropriate groups.

Newsgroups:

This contains the newsgroup or newsgroups to which the message will be posted. If you put more than one group in, separate the names with commas. Only one copy of the posting will be sent, but it will be listed in all the groups mentioned.

Subject:

The subject of the posting. If you're changing the subject of a follow-up, the convention is to include the old subject in brackets, after "was:". So a follow-up to a posting called "Pubs in London" could be "Firkin Pubs (was: Pubs in London)".

Email To:

If you put an eMail address or addresses in this field, the message will also be eMailed to them (so you can be sure that the original author sees it, for example).

 If you put "poster" in this field, follow-ups will be eMailed to you (the poster).

Followup-To:

If your posting is followed up, this group will be filled in as the default group to post to. So, if you're putting a request about London Pubs to a number of groups, but want all follow-ups to go to alt.beer, put alt.beer in the Followup-To field.

Distribution:

This field doesn't always work, but is worth filling in for politeness. It limits how far the posting will be passed on to news servers. If your posting isn't relevant outside UK, put in a distribution of "uk".

Expires:

News servers will normally decide for themselves when to expire articles. You can override this by putting a date in this field (so you can make a posting expire at Christmas if it hasn't already, say).

Binary Attachments

Be *very* suspicious of program files posted to news groups - it's a common way for viruses to be distributed. If you have to, run a virus checker on the file *before* you run it.

Some newsgroups, especially those with "binary" in their title, carry postings with "binary attachments". Attachments are files, usually images or sounds but sometimes executable programs, which could not normally be posted to a newsgroup.

Binary attachments are encoded using a system called UUencode which lets them be posted. News has quite strict limits to the length of an individual posting, so binaries are often split into a number of files.

You can recognise a binary attachment because it looks like this (apparently gibberish).

1 Select any of the files which makes up the binary.

2 Press the "Decode Binaries" button.

3 Wait while Agent downloads all the files that make up the binary. This can take a while.

4 The binary file is placed on your hard disk. If you have used Windows to assign an application for the file type in question, Agent will launch that application. If not, you can do it by hand.

Happy Thanksgiving!

Signature Files

Just like Eudora (see Chapter Four), Agent allows you to define a signature which will be placed automatically at the end of your postings.

Since you often need to present a different image in the `comp` groups than you would in an `alt` group (see later what these groups are), Agent allows you to define a number of different signatures.

To edit your signature settings, select "Signatures..." from the "Options" menu.

Your different signatures are listed in this box.

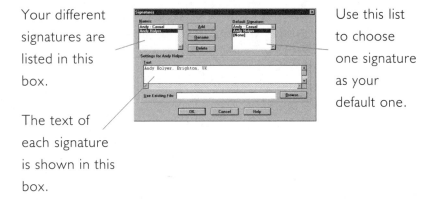

Use this list to choose one signature as your default one.

The text of each signature is shown in this box.

Warning

I've said this before, but it's worth stressing again. It can be very tempting to use a big, fancy signature with your address, phone and fax numbers, star sign, quote from Wayne's World and a little ASCII picture of Garfield. Please don't. I've been there, I've done it, and take it from me, you'll only regret it in the morning.

In the world of signature files, less is definitely more. On *no* account should your signature file be more than four lines *ever*.

Purging & Expiry

Purging

You can control the circumstances under which Agent clears old messages from your hard disk. Agent allows you to define a default behaviour for all groups, and different behaviour for individual groups. The dialogue box you get is identical in either case.

1 Select either "Properties for Selected Groups" or "Default Properties for All Groups" from the "Group" menu.

2 Select "What to Purge".

3 Depending on how much disk space you can spare, select one of these options.

4 Make any other changes you may want (you can always tweak this later).

5 Select "When to Purge".

6 Select the options you wish. I set Agent to purge every time I fetch new headers, and every time I quit.

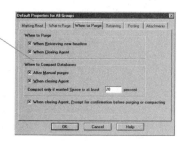

Expiry

A full news feed is currently about 150 Megabytes a day, and doubles every few months. Because of this, news servers have to continually clear out old postings to make space for new ones. This process is called expiry.

You have no control over expiry: it's done by your provider as part of the housekeeping of their system. However, it can be a bit startling when you first encounter it, so you should know what's going on.

More than half the whole Usenet feed consists of the alt groups (see later). Of this, the vast majority is taken up by `alt.binaries`. For this reason, most providers put a very short expiry on these groups, often only a day or two. So if you don't read news for a few days, you could miss articles in these groups entirely.

The more serious groups are often kept longer, between a couple of weeks and a month or so. That way, you're less likely to miss something if you're away. Longest of all are usually the provider's own local groups.

It's worth bearing in mind that different providers may have different expiry times, so just because a message is still on *your* local news server doesn't mean that it's still on the news server of your friend, who has a different provider.

The final decision on expiry is up to the administrator of the news server, but you can make suggestions for individual postings by using the "Expires:" header. So, if you've posted an announcement for an event, it's worth setting the expiry of the event to be the day after it occurs. That way, you won't get people seeing it the day after it happens, either.

Newsgroups

Newsgroups are arranged in a hierarchy of domains in the same sort of way as Internet addresses: however in an Internet address as you read from left to right, the domains get larger, whereas a newsgroup starts with the most general domain and gets more and more specific.

For example, the newsgroup `comp.sys.ibm.pc` is part of the `comp` hierarchy, which is generally to do with computers. The `sys` identifies it as being concerned with a specific computer system, rather than (say) a programming language; the `ibm` and the `pc` elements identify it as covering PCs and compatibles (there are in fact a number of groups within the `comp.sys.ibm.pc` hierarchy, each with a different purpose).

At first glance, there are a bewildering number of newsgroups: even if you just look at the top-level categories there seem to be thousands of categories. However, many hierarchies on a commercial news server are local newsgroups for foreign countries or for universities, and hence are of little interest (for example any group beginning with `za` is local to South Africa, and so of little day-to-day interest except to expatriates). Almost all newsgroups that you will be interested in fall under about eight headings.

REMEMBER

Where I use a "*" in the name of a news group, it means the same as you would use it in DOS. So, news.* means "all the newsgroups beginning with news....".

news.*: how Usenet is run

The newsgroups which begin with `news.` deal with the administration of the Usenet system. New groups are discussed on `news.config`: New groups are announced on `news.announce`. It's unlikely that you will have much reason to read `news.*` groups, and even less reason to take part in discussions, but there is one `news.*` group which you should look at.

The group `news.announce.newusers` carries a range of Frequently Asked Question lists aimed at new users.

The "Big Five"

The core of Usenet consist of five hierarchies of newsgroups, and are where most of the serious discussion is to be found. These five topics were historically the first groups to be created: some of them have been going for over fifteen years now.

The Big Five groups are far more controlled than the rest of Usenet. Many of the groups are moderated (see the section later in this chapter), which cuts out off-topic postings. There are strict controls on the creation of newsgroups, unlike other areas of Usenet: a long and involved process of proposal, debate and finally an Internet-wide vote is necessary.

Each of the Big Five groups is described separately below.

comp.*: Computing groups

HANDY TIP

Some of the theory-based comp.* groups are read by leading names in their subjects: for example, a common poster to comp.ai is John McCarthy, one of the founding fathers of Artificial Intelligence.

Once upon a time, everybody on the Internet worked with computers. Now only 60% do - and the figure is dropping by the day. So, historically, the first groups set up were in the comp.* hierarchy.

In these groups you will find all sorts of things which are directly related to computers: discussion of the finer points of programming languages (see, for example `comp.lang.c`); advice on operating systems (`comp.os.ms-dos.*`); leading-edge academic work (`comp.ai.*`).

For readers of this book, the most useful comp groups will probably be `comp.sys.ibm.pc.*`, where you can find advice from all over the world about using and setting up IBM-compatible PCs.

sci.*: Science

The `sci.*` newsgroups are also a relic of the early days of Usenet. They cover sciences other than computer science. If you are interested in science, they can be quite interesting: the `sci.aeronautics.*` and `sci.space.*` groups provide up-to-the-minute information about aircraft and about space science, for example. Mostly these groups are the haunts of specialists in their particular fields.

One sci group does merit special attention. The group `sci.skeptic` is one of the main discussion areas for the Skeptics movement. The Skeptics are a group of (mostly) scientists who investigate cases of pseudo-science (psychic powers, UFOs, astrology etc.), and (mostly) debunk them.

Make of this what you will (personally, I'm on the side of the skeptics), but the thing that makes this group worth reading is the fact that it acts as a magnet for Psychic investigators, mediums, and UFO fans who are determined to prove these "godless, unbelieving scientists" wrong. The ensuing arguments are rarely conclusive, but often hilarious. If you're really lucky, someone will post an account of his last trip to Sirius on a UFO.

rec.*: Recreation

The recreation groups cover a wide range of entertainment topics.

The `rec.arts` hierarchy covers books, theatre, cinema and a wide range of other topics. `rec.auto.*` deals with cars, `rec.aviation.misc` with private aircraft. The `rec.food.*` groups often contain interesting recipes - in fact there are a number of recipe books available on the Internet made up of recipes found here.

There is a bewildering range of groups under the `rec.music.*` hierarchy. Many of these groups have a lot of traffic (hundreds of messages per day), so think before you join too many. Of note are `rec.music.misc`, the main group, `rec.music.gdead` (about the Grateful

Dead), which has contributions from members of the band, and `rec.music.gaffa`, the Kate Bush list. I read the last of these for a period, but found it altogether too fawning - there's a certain type of fan who is just a bit too much, and in my opinion `rec.music.gaffa` is made up of these.

The `rec.*` groups are usually fairly gentle and helpful, and are a good place for a beginner (generally nobody will be too rude to you if you say the wrong thing). Follow the local habits, though - the regulars don't take too kindly to deliberate rudeness. There was a celebrated occasion a couple of years ago when the regulars on `alt.tasteless` (who start at sick humour and go on from there) decided to "invade" `rec.pets.cats` (which is as you can imagine a very gentle and serious group). The ensuing scenes were in some ways funny, but were also very unpleasant to some, and the locals are still a bit sensitive about the whole affair.

There are several `rec.*` groups which carry reviews (`rec.arts.movies.reviews`, `rec.arts.books.reviews` etc.). These are well worth following, since the reviews are by normal Internet users (i.e. probably with similar taste to you), rather than by journalists. They're a brilliant way to be able to spout off about the latest Hollywood movies before anyone in the UK even knows they're coming out.

One thing to bear in mind: The `rec.*` groups, like most of Usenet and indeed the Internet itself, are heavily US-dominated. `rec.sport.football` is about American football. To discuss how Liverpool are doing, see `rec.sport.soccer` - and still don't be surprised if a lot of the people there have never heard of Paul Gascoigne. The same cautions apply to `rec.food.drink.beer` - you do get tired of people asking "what does Guinness taste like?" after a few weeks.

misc.*: Miscellaneous

The `misc.*` groups were created in the early days of Usenet as the repository of everything which didn't have a good home anywhere else. Nowadays it is something of the haunted gallery of Usenet, although there are a few gems: `misc.misc` is *the* definitive misc group (although for us, `uk.misc` is more relevant), and there are useful things in `misc.business.*` and `misc.consumers.*`.

There is a thriving trade going on in `misc.forsale.*`, where you can often find bargains (though most of the posters are from the wrong side of the Atlantic - look in `uk.misc` for stuff you can really buy).

All is worth a look once in a while, but essentially of passing interest (though in looking through the groups for this book I stumbled on `misc.news.bosnia`, which is fascinating).

soc.*: Social

The `soc.*` groups, as their name implies, cover social topics. In general, this means social as in "with respect to society", rather then social as in "friendly", though some soc groups are very friendly. Others, however, are a good deal less cordial.

The largest soc subsection is the `soc.culture.*` hierarchy. These groups cover the society and issues of foreign countries. Note that, since Usenet is US-based, we count as a foreign country: there exists `soc.culture.british`, `soc.culture.welsh` and `soc.culture.scottish`. I find `soc.culture.british` quite interesting, though a lot of the posters are US Anglophiles, and you do often get questions like "so, how often do you meet Lady Di?", or "why do you drink warm beer?".

Some of the `soc.culture.*` groups can be quite contentious: there was a protracted fight a year or two ago over the creation of `soc.culture.tibet` (there are a surprising number of mainland Chinese studying at western universities, and they stick together: in the official Chinese view "there's no such country as Tibet". The more restrained `soc.culture` groups are really useful if you're planning a holiday, and want to know what the natives think of the places your travel agent has suggested.

Another very valuable set of soc groups is the `soc.support.*` hierarchy. This covers a range of mainly long-term and non-life-threatening illnesses (for example `soc.support.depression`) and for sufferers and their relatives this can be a lifeline.

One other `soc.*` group needs explanation. The group which covers gay issues is called `soc.motss`: "motss" stands for "member of the same sex" - there also exist the acronyms "motos" (member of the opposite sex) and "motas" (member of the appropriate sex) - though these don't have their own soc groups.

alt.*: The Alternative groups

Welcome to amateur hour. The `alt.*` groups appeared after the "Big Five" had been established. There is no control whatsoever over the creation of alt groups: Pretty much anyone can create them: unfortunately, anyone can delete them, too.

The alt hierarchy has become one of the most active areas of Usenet. There are thousands of groups, ranging from the serious (`alt.music.the-doors`) to the incredibly silly (`alt.swedish.chef.bork.bork.bork`). Many of the conventions and catch-phrases of the Internet evolved in the alt groups. It can also be an intimidating place for the unwary.

It's difficult to read about the Internet for very long without coming up against the subject of sex. Yes, there are sex and drugs on the Internet, and the alt groups are where you'll find them. In fact, when the alt hierarchy was first established the first group established was `alt.sex`. The group `alt.drugs` was the second, followed the next day by `alt.rock-n-roll` - "for symmetry" as the original creator put it.

HANDY TIP

Many groups have a "Frequently Asked Questions" list, which consists of those questions which arise over and over again and puts them together in one place. A FAQ is usually posted to the group every few weeks, and is often also available by FTP.

The `alt.sex.*` and `alt.drugs.*` groups are in fact a lot less extreme than they first appear. The `alt.sex.binaries.*` groups do have pornographic pictures, but they reflect their main audience - US undergraduates. There is the occasional shocker, but in most cases a copy of Playboy is far more revealing. Many of the other groups are quite responsible - `alt.drugs` mainly consists of advice on the effects and legality of drugs, and the `alt.sex` FAQ is a very responsible attempt to dispel myths about sex. It's certainly more useful than The Joy of Sex.

The alt groups have other things to offer besides onanism. The `alt.fan` groups are variable but can be quite amusing: for example `alt.fan.pratchett`, which deals with the works of Terry Pratchett sometimes features the man himself as a correspondent. A spin-off from this group, The Annotated Pratchett, is worth acquiring if you read his books (the fact that I wrote a few bits of this should in no way influence your decision).

A favourite alt group of mine is `alt.folklore.urban`. Did you ever hear the story of the family on holiday in Spain when their grandmother died? They couldn't afford to fly her back, so they strapped her to the roof rack of their car. All was fine, until they stopped in a French motorway service station, and their car was stolen, along with grandma... Stories like this are called urban legends, and besides the column in the Guardian every Saturday, have been examined in a very funny series of books by a professor of folklore called Jan Harald Brunvand. The group `alt.folklore.urban` examines these stories, and in particular attempts to confirm or refute new stories. Along the way, they have taken on tracing the source of well-known phrases and of examining common scientific fallacies (as I write there is an argument going on as to whether glass is or is not a liquid). As the group as a whole puts it, "it's a great place to get a reality check on anything that 'a friend' told you, or to compare notes about odd things." Along the way, AFU has acquired a whole collection of in-jokes which makes it pretty opaque the first time you encounter it: stick with it - all will soon become clear.

Equally strange, from a different angle is `alt.fan.warlord`. When you first start to use the Internet, an early discovery is that signature files can be used for a wide variety of things beyond just identifying yourself. Borders, quotes, funny lines and pictures made from ASCII characters are popular (the Starship Enterprise is a common topic for these pictures).

A large signature can be quite fun the first time you see it, but it can get tiresome if it's posted over and over again. It's especially annoying if you pay for your connection (as many of us do these days) and the signature is actually bigger than the message sent.

This process of signature inflation reached its nadir in a group devoted to a fantasy game called Warlord. ASCII representations of swords were particularly popular. In response to this, the group `alt.fan.warlord` was created. The group is devoted to displaying examples of offending signatures (posted from other Usenet groups) and parodying them. Some of the abbreviations used by warlorders can be pretty obscure, but once you get the idea, it can be hilarious. And, it teaches you to keep that signature small.

uk.*: The UK's own groups

Most of Usenet is international in scope. In practice this means that it is overwhelmingly dominated by Americans. Reflecting this, every country outside of the USA has its own set of newsgroups, most of which rarely get outside their own borders. This explains many of the obscure group names you will see on the full group list: for example, the `za.*` groups are local to South Africa (and many of them are in Afrikaans, to make things worse).

The UK's local groups all (not surprisingly) begin with
uk.*. At the centre is uk.misc. Very high traffic, and
terribly long-winded at times, uk.misc should be checked
out from time to time. The group uk.politics is horrid
to download, since it's so big, but can be fascinating,
especially since there are now MPs from all three major
parties posting to it regularly. uk.jobs.* and
uk.forsale speak for themselves.

There are a few uk-related groups in other areas of Usenet,
but bear in mind that they will be full of expats and
Anglophiles. rec.arts.tv.uk suffers from the fact that
English television is shown abroad years behind us: there
was an occasion when the eMail address of Points of View
was revealed in this group, and Anne Robinson was
bemused to receive hundreds of messages from Americans
asking if there were any plans for another series of "Fawlty
Towers" or "Are You Being Served?".

Local groups

In addition to the national and global news groups, most
Internet providers have a few groups specific to
themselves. For example, Pavilion's groups are all called
pavilion.*, and centre on pavilion.misc. Demon's
local groups are carried by quite a few news servers, and
have become a de facto alternative UK hierarchy. In
particular, the demon.support.* groups provide useful
guidance in troubleshooting your Internet connection.

Set Task: Asking for Help

If you've got a technical problem, Usenet news can be one of the best source of advice. There are thousands of people all over the world who read the `comp` groups, and many of them will have encountered your problem before and will be glad to help. In this section I'll describe the steps you should go through when you have a problem with your computer.

1 Define your problem. You're much more likely to get help, and the help will probably be of better quality, if you do all the donkey work of looking up version numbers etc. *before* you ask for help. "My modem is playing up. What's wrong?" is not likely to get any useful replies. "I've got a US Robotics Sportster 28.8 and when I try to drive it at 57,600 baud from my 150Mhz. Pentium under Windows 95..." has a better chance of getting a response. Before you put together your request you should know: the spec of your computer (processor, speed, memory, if necessary BIOS versions etc.); all the software involved, and (where relevant) the version numbers; a concise definition of the problem with details, if possible, of how it can be reproduced.

2 Choose the group to which you should go for help. It will probably be one of the `comp.sys.ibm.pc.*` groups, but make sure you choose the right one - a request to an inappropriate group will not be favourably received. In the case of the problem above, the appropriate group is `comp.sys.ibm.hardware.comm`.

3 Check your chosen group to make sure that your question hasn't come up recently. You find that the same problems crop up over and over again, and yours may be one of them. At the very least, look through all postings from the group that are available. If the group keeps a FAQ, check it to see that your problem isn't in it.

4 Compose your request for help. Be polite - the people out there don't *have* to help you, they're doing you a favour if they answer. Check all the headers - in particular, check that your eMail address is correct. If people find that a reply to you bounces, they won't bother to track you down. If you don't normally read the group in question, finish by saying "Please reply directly to me, and I'll summarize and report to this group".

5 If you've promised to summarise and post, *make sure you do it*. Otherwise people will be less inclined to help you again.

6 Post your message. Then wait. Don't worry if you don't get a reply for a couple of days - even nowadays, it takes about a week for a posting to make it all the way round the world.

CHAPTER SIX

File Transfer Protocol

File Transfer Protocol (FTP) allows you to copy files across the Internet. In particular, it gives you access to a wide range of software, documents, and image files. This chapter shows you how to use FTP.

Covers

Introduction

We can all use more software than we've already got. On the Internet, there is a wide range of software freely available. You just have to download it.

You copy files over the Internet using File Transfer Protocol, or FTP for short. There are a number of ways to use FTP. Most World Wide Web browsers will handle FTP, but since they weren't designed for this purpose, they don't perform as well as a dedicated program.

In this chapter I'll show you how to use WS FTP, a Windows program designed specifically for FTP.

Freeware and Shareware

Most of the software that you find on the Internet is freeware or shareware. This means that you don't need to pay any money in order to set up and run the program: in the case of shareware you should pay some money if you want to use the software for long-term.

Freeware comes in a couple of categories. Some software is fully in the public domain: you can use this totally freely, give copies to your friends, more or less what you want. The only limitation with public domain software is that it often forbids you from charging for it, except for a small charge for the floppy disk it comes on. This can be tricky if you're selling some software which you've produced, but which uses a public domain editor, for example.

A lot of recent software is commercial, but is available for "evaluation" to individuals. Netscape is an example of this: most of their income is from selling their server software, so it's obviously in their interest to make sure that the browsing software is used by as many people as possible. Licensed software like this often has significant limitations on how you can pass it on.

Shareware is free to try, but if you want to use it regularly, then you should pay for it. This is usually pretty cheap - £10 or so is about average, but a lot of people never bother to register their shareware.

There are a number of tricks to induce you to register shareware. Sometimes the free version is limited in some way (this is called "crippleware"). Other packages will only work for a month, and disables itself if you haven't registered in that time. Others give you a printed manual, free upgrades to new versions, or telephone support when you register.

One of my favourite shareware schemes is a cheap one: the author just wants to know that the program's being used, so he asks you to send him a postcard from wherever you live.

Anonymous FTP

FTP was originally devised to allow you to copy files between machines you had accounts on. To copy files, you had to have a username and password on the remote machine.

This would obviously not work for public archives, so anonymous FTP was invented.

When you connect to an FTP server, you are asked for a username. For anonymous FTP, enter "anonymous" or "ftp" as the username. If an anonymous connection is accepted, enter your eMail address as the password. This is logged to a file, so that the administrator of the FTP archive can see who has accessed the site.

Because of the load it imposes on the system, there is often a strict limit on the number of anonymous FTP sessions which are allowed at one time. If the server is busy, you may find your connection refused: if so, try again later, or try a different archive. It's worth bearing in mind the time of day (especially the time of day at the other end). The quietest time is usually the very early morning, so you'll be most likely to get into a U.S. archive if you try to connect before 2p.m. in the UK - that's before 8a.m. in the USA.

WS FTP: an FTP Client

As I said before, you can use Netscape to access anonymous FTP archives, but I find it's more trouble than it's worth, especially for large files. WS FTP is a Windows program specifically designed to handle FTP. It's more reliable, and also transfers slightly faster.

If you need to do non-anonymous FTP (for example, if you run a WWW site and need to update the pages), you can't use Netscape: you have to use a dedicated FTP client.

This is WS FTP's main window:

The top boxes show directories.

The lower boxes show files.

This window contains a log of the current session.

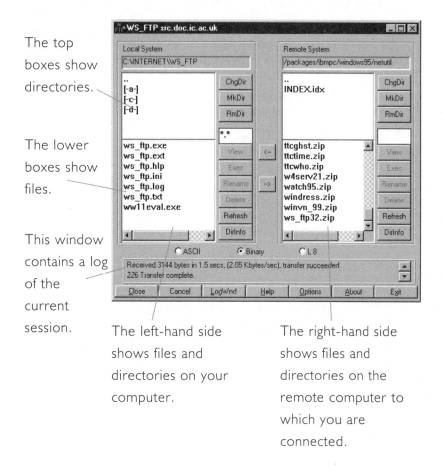

The left-hand side shows files and directories on your computer.

The right-hand side shows files and directories on the remote computer to which you are connected.

Opening an FTP Connection

When you run WS FTP, or press the "Connect" button you will see this dialogue box:

HANDY TIP

WS FTP comes with a set of useful FTP sites already set up.

| You can give each remote site a name: put it in this box.

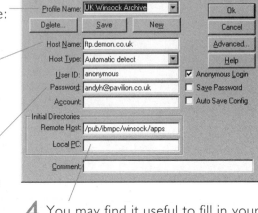

2 Put the address in this box.

3 Either: fill in your username and password, or click on the Anonymous Login check box.

4 You may find it useful to fill in your initial and remote pathnames (that is, your location on local and remote systems) in these boxes.

5 Finally, press OK, and WS FTP will try and connect to the remote site.

Putting or Fetching Files

Once you are able to connect to the remote system, you can fetch files.

1 WS FTP displays two file selectors. Use the left file selector to choose where you want to put the file you download.

FTP archives often have files called "README.TXT" or "INDEX.TXT" which will tell you what the files in the archives are.

2 Use the right file selector to find the file you want to download or upload.

3 Press either the [<--] button (if you want to download) or the [-->] button (if you want to upload) to start the transfer.

4 You will see a window like this appear: wait until the stripe has gone all the way across.

If a transfer stops in the middle, it may not cancel by itself. Watch the modem lights - if there's no activity for 20 seconds, you may need to press the Cancel button.

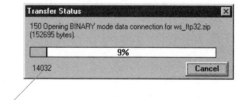

This is the total number of bytes transferred.

Compressed Files

Usually, if you fetch a program by FTP you will not be able to use it immediately. Most programs are stored as a compressed archive file. There are two reasons for this. Firstly, most software packages consist of more than one file - besides the .exe, there will be manuals, help files etc. An archive file means that you've only got one thing to download, and you won't miss anything. Secondly, archive files are compressed, so they save space on the FTP archive, and they take you less time to transfer. So, everyone wins.

There are a number of different sorts of archive files - you can tell which type by looking at the file type. On a PC, the most common is the Zip format.

To extract the files from a Zip archive, you need suitable software. There is a range of programs which allow you to do this: the most basic is PKUNZIP.EXE, which runs under DOS, but there are a number of Windows programs to do the same job. WinZip is good: if you are running Windows 95, then you'll find Zip Explorer easy.

CHAPTER SEVEN

Telnet

Telnet allows you to open a command line connection to a remote computer. This chapter shows you how to use Telnet to access library catalogues and MUDs, on-line multi-player games.

Covers

Introduction

Once upon a time, not that long ago, computers did not have a windows-and-mouse interface. If you wanted to use a computer, you used a character-based interface.

When the Internet appeared, people wanted to be able to operate a computer at a distance, without having to use a terminal directly connected to the computer. This service is called Telnet.

In some ways, Telnet is one of the less interesting Internet services. You simply get a command line interface into the machine you connect to. No graphics, no sound (except for the occasional beep).

There are a couple of reasons for using Telnet. Firstly, you may actually need to work on a machine at a distance. If you're a University Computer Science Student, you can log onto your department computer system and do your homework without having to go into the lab (and pay a bus fare/leave your children/etc.). There are a lot of older information services available on the Internet which have a command line interface. The most useful of these are library catalogues - for example, most UK universities are on-line. You can't actually read the books, but it still has its uses.

The other use is a way of life on its own. This is the world of MUDs and MOOs, and has its own section later in this chapter.

Ewan: a Telnet Application

To use Telnet, you need a Telnet application. You can't use the normal Windows Terminal program, because that just takes over the modem, and you're already using that to run the TCP/IP protocol. There are only a couple of Telnet programs around, since it's not exactly a growing service. Of these, the best is called Ewan.

 If the system you connect to asks you for the "terminal type", answer "VT100" - Ewan emulates this, and it's a very common terminal type.

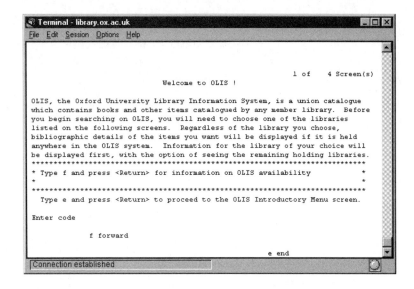

Telnet applications don't have many controls: there's the light in the bottom right-hand corner which tells you if you've got a connection or not (it turns green when the connection is up). You can define a list of connections you use regularly, and define any special cases for these (like a different keyboard layout). You can log data to a file, or cut and paste from the terminal window. Other than that, you've got a terminal, you type into it and it types back at you.

Library Catalogues

Virtually all university libraries in the UK have a computerised catalogue, and the vast majority of these are accessible via the Internet. The same is also true for foreign universities. Most of these services are listed on a service called "Hytelnet": A listing of UK libraries can be found by pointing in Netscape at
`http://www.cam.ac.uk/Hytelnet/uk0/uk000.html`

In order to run a Telnet session directly from Netscape, you'll need to tell Netscape where your copy of Ewan is.

1 In Netscape, select "General Preferences" from the "Options" menu.

2 Use "Browse" to find your copy of Ewan in the "Telnet Application" box.

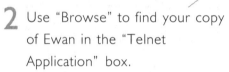

Public libraries are slower in connecting to the Internet, and few have their catalogues on-line. Some have WWW pages, though. To find out more, point your Web browser at
`http://dspace.dial.pipex.com/town/square/ac940/ukpublib.html`

The British Library has its own on-line service, but in order to use the catalogue you need to register at a cost of £85 per year. For more details, point your Web browser at
`http://portico.bl.uk/`

Multi-User Dungeons

In the beginning there was Adventure. In the early seventies, Will Crowther produced this game, based on his experience of Potholing, and on the role-playing game Dungeons and Dragons. It became one of the standard bits of free software given away with a DEC computer, and hence became popular in universities, who bought lots of DECs. In the eighties there were quite a lot of adventures available for home computers, notably a series produced by Infocom (which are still available at low price if you look around).

In 1979 two undergraduates at the University of Essex produced MUD, a multi-player version of adventure which could be played over computer networks. It quickly gained a following not just amongst people at Essex, but also around the world. With the spread of the Internet, several refined versions were produced and today there are dozens of MUDs running.

If you're used to modern computer games, the first sight of a MUD is disappointing. There are no graphics; you are given a (verbal) description of your character's location and can issue short commands allowing you to move around, pick up and use objects, open doors etc.

The real appeal of a MUD is the fact that there are other people using it at the same time. This provides a social element - indeed many MUDs have totally lost their sword-and-sorcery background, and have become a purely social experience.

Each player takes on a character. This allows you to present yourself pretty much as you wish: if you want to appear to be the opposite sex, so be it. As your character does things your abilities grow, until eventually you reach "wizard" rank which allows you to change the game, doing things to other players and building new parts of the world.

Some people, when they discover MUD, do little else. It is true that to get anywhere in a MUD you need a *lot* of free time - to get to a serious level you need to spend hours on-line. For this reason I have only ever dabbled in playing MUDs, but I can see the appeal.

There are at least three complete families of MUDs around at the moment, based on the software used to construct them. There are those games based on the MUD code and on LPMud, a refinement; these stay close to the original fantasy setting. There are what are called MUCKs, which tend to aim towards building and socialising, and MOOs which are... just plain odd, basically.

You access a MUD by Telnetting to the machine which runs it. At this point you are asked to sign in your character, and then you can carry on with the action.

If you'd like to find out more about MUDs point your Web browser at
`http://www.yahoo.com/Recreation/Games/Internet_Games/`
`MUDs_MUSHes_MOOs_etc_/`

There are lots of links! Oh, and if you're interested in this sort of game, definitely check out
`http://www.avalon-rpg.com/`

CHAPTER EIGHT

Internet Relay Chat

Internet Relay Chat allows you to chat in real time to other Internet users. This chapter describes IRC and shows you how to get started.

Covers

Introduction

Internet Relay Chat ("IRC" for short) is the CB Radio of the 'Net. You can join one or more "channels" and chat real-time to other people - who can be all over the world (though obviously local time does have an effect here).

The interface of IRC is very basic. All communication is textual (you certainly get used to typing quickly), and for a long time you used to have to give commands (to join or leave channels etc.) textually, too. There are now IRC client programs appearing which allow a bit more of a point-and-click approach, but it's still pretty basic.

IRC is one of those services that people either love or hate. On the plus side, it's an extremely immediate experience, and the feeling of bonding to other people can be very strong. On the other hand, at its worst, IRC can be one of the most trivial things you're likely to encounter on the Internet, a place where the trivial is pretty commonplace.

There are a very few occasions when IRC has a practical use. There were stories that during the Gulf War there were IRC sessions which reported on the war first-hand; some Israelis put computers with modems in their sealed rooms and spent the time during air raids on the 'Net (well, I suppose it keeps your mind off things...).

Occasionally you get celebrities taking part in "on-line phone-ins" on IRC, in which any number of fans can log on to an IRC channel and bombard the celebrity with questions. On the whole, though, if IRC appeals to you, good luck. If it's not your sort of thing, I can't honestly say you'll be missing much.

mIRC: an IRC Client

It's possible to connect to IRC using Telnet, though it's not for the innocent: the command syntax is a bit hairy. A better approach for the beginner is a dedicated IRC client like mIRC.

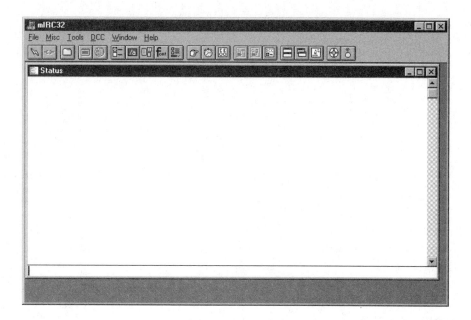

At first sight, mIRC is pretty sparse. You've got a row of buttons, which control various administrative operations, and one window, the status window.

The status window displays your link to your local *IRC server* (there are IRC servers all over the world, passing IRC data from one to another). Any messages from the server will be displayed in this window.

When you join a channel, a new window like this one is opened. You can join as many channels as you like: each of them will have their own window.

Connecting to Your Server

To use IRC you first have to connect to your nearest IRC server. As I said before, there are IRC servers all over the Internet. There are a couple in the UK: the best one to use is generally the one run by Demon Internet, `irc.demon.co.uk`.

Once you've configured your client, you can connect by just pressing the button, but the first time you have to do this:

1 Select "Setup" from the "File" menu (or press the ⬚ button).

HANDY TIP

You can connect to whichever IRC server you want, but you'll get better performance if you choose one close to you. In the UK, the best one to use is irc.demon.co.uk.

2 Fill in your details in these boxes. You can choose whatever you want for a nickname, but if there's already one in use, it'll be rejected, so think of a second choice.

3 Choose an IRC server either by typing in a name, or by selecting one from the list.

4 Press this button. You should see a dialogue in the Status window:

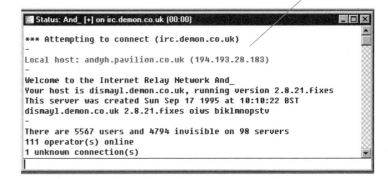

Joining Channels

To actually talk to people, you need to join one or more channels.

1 Click on the button.

All IRC channel names are written with a "#" character at the beginning.

2 Select a channel, either from the list or by typing it in the box.

3 To see who is on the channel, press "Names". The list will appear in the status window.

4 To join the channel, press "Join". A new window will open.

The window header shows the channel name, and its current subject.

The action of the channel appears in this box.

These are the people on the channel. Those with an "@" by their names have Operator status (see later).

Type your messages in this box at the bottom.

Listing Channels

You can get mIRC to list all the channels currently on IRC.

1 Press the 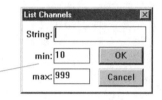 button.

2 You can choose groups which match a string, and those with at least, and less than a particular number of people. Fill in this dialogue box appropriately.

List Channels	
String:	
min:	10
max:	999

OK Cancel

 BEWARE

Fetching the channel list takes quite a while - there are nearly 3,000 of them, and while it's being fetched everything else stops. So don't try it too often.

3 After a while this window will be displayed.

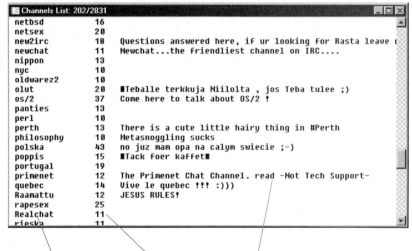

Channels List: 202/2831

netbsd	16	
netsex	20	
new2irc	18	Questions answered here, if ur looking for Rasta leave
newchat	11	Newchat...the friendliest channel on IRC....
nippon	13	
nyc	10	
oldwarez2	10	
olut	20	∎Teballe terkkuja Niilolta , jos Teba tulee ;)
os/2	37	Come here to talk about OS/2 !
panties	13	
perl	10	
perth	13	There is a cute little hairy thing in #Perth
philosophy	10	Metasnoggling sucks
polska	43	no juz mam opa na calym swiecie ;-)
poppis	15	∎Tack foer kaffet∎
portugal	19	
primenet	12	The Primenet Chat Channel. read -Not Tech Support-
quebec	14	Uive le quebec !!! :)))
Raamattu	12	JESUS RULES!
rapesex	25	
Realchat	11	
rieska	11	

The name of the channel.   The number of people on it at the moment.   Each channel's current subject.

Talking and Actions

This is where it begins to get complicated. IRC was invented by programmers, and the skeleton is still quite visible, especially in the case of talking on a channel. Also, mIRC can be customised almost completely - especially the pop-up menus: don't be surprised if your pop-ups look nothing like the ones I show.

To say something in a channel, just type it in the box at the bottom and hit the Enter key; it will appear in the main window, marked with your Nickname. All messages sent to a channel are seen by everyone on it.

You can also do what is called an *action;* To do this, type "/me" followed by what you do. For example, my Nickname is "And_". If I type "/me cheers", then the line "And_ cheers" will appear in the main window.

REMEMBER

You can have as many channel or chat windows open at once as you like - but it can get a bit confusing after about four or five!

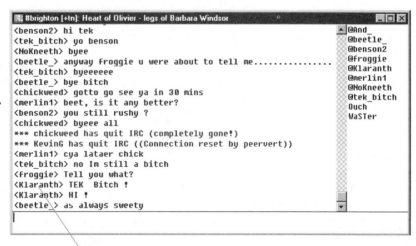

Each message sent to a channel is marked by that person's Nickname.

Chat Mode

As well as the general conversation in a channel, you can open one-to-one discussions with someone. These are only seen by the two of you involved in the session.

1 Double-click on the entry in the list of Nicknames of the person you wish to talk to.

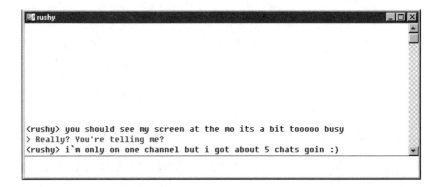

2 A new window will open. You can talk, perform actions, and type any other IRC commands just like in a channel window, but stuff in this window will only be seen by the two of you.

Nicknames

When you connect to IRC, you are asked to choose a *Nickname,* or "Nick" for short. This is rather like a handle on CB radio, and the only requirement is that nobody else on IRC is using it. If someone has already got your Nick, the IRC server will ask you for a different one. This is why mIRC asks you for a second choice of Nickname.

You can change your Nickname at any time during a session (with the limitation that it must be unique). To do this type "/nick *(whatever your new nickname is)*". People sometimes do this to indicate a change of mood.

You can find out about the owner of a Nickname by using the "/whois" command or, in mIRC by using the popup menus.

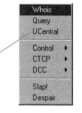

I Select a Nickname from the Nickname list.

2 Click with *the right mouse button* on the name. You will see this pop-up menu.

You may not get all the details you want from these commands. **Not all systems provide all information, and** *there's nothing to ensure that people tell the truth.* **It's worth being careful.**

3 If you select "Whois" then details of that Nickname will be shown in the control window. If you select "UCentral" then you will see this window appear.

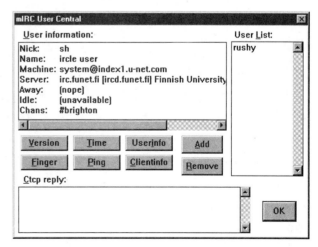

Operator Mode

If you have Operator mode over a channel, the world (or at least the channel) is your mollusc. You can change the subject of a channel. You can kick people out of a channel if they annoy you. You can ban people from a channel so that they can't rejoin it. You can make a channel private, so that people have to be invited to join it. You can set a channel so that only messages you allow will appear. You can even make a channel secret, so it doesn't show up on the master list of channels.

The only problem with this is that it's not that easy to gain Operator mode. There are two ways: if you're the first person in a channel, then you're the Operator - but then you're all alone. Or, you can get someone who is already an Operator to give you Op's status. Needless to say, Operators only pass this on to their friends.

Assuming you're lucky enough to be given Operator status, changing channel details is easy in mIRC:

Double-click in the channel window. You will see this dialogue box:

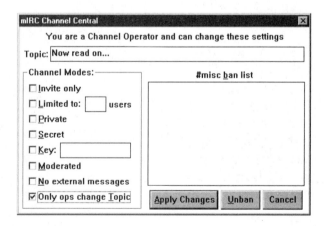

2 As Operator, you can change any of these options: As a Non-Operator, you can read them, but can't change them.

CHAPTER NINE

Being a Good Citizen

So far, this book has looked at the mechanics of accessing the Internet. To a very large degree, however, the Internet is a social entity (a small nation of over 40 million people), and you need to know about the way things are done there, as well as consider some of the risks involved.

Covers

Security

People have a number of concerns about the security implications of connecting to the Internet. One of the first is to do with hackers breaking into their computer. This is of particular concern to companies keeping confidential information on their machines.

In general, there isn't much to worry about here. The Internet software which is supplied by most Internet providers (and which has been described in this book) only sets your machine up to read from the Internet, and does not allow anyone to get in from outside. Most companies are far more at risk of their machines being stolen or damaged accidentally (a few days before I wrote this, my next-door neighbour had his computer struck by lightning, and lost all his accounts and business records).

To allow an outsider to connect to a machine on the Internet, it is necessary for a server program to be running on your machine. There are Internet servers available for the Windows environment, but they're not usually worth running over a dial-up connection - they'll only be available while you're dialled in.

HANDY TIP **Server programs are often referred to as "daemons", so the name of the programs involved often have a "d" on the end. For example, a Telnet daemon is called "telnetd".**

If you are inclined to run an Internet server - say on your departmental file server - then these security issues become a great deal more serious. In this case you should begin seriously thinking about employing someone specifically to run the service and to see to its security. The security measures necessary are beyond the scope of this book. There are a number of more technical books on Internet security, which you should consult.

A more general worry is over the security of eMail. This is something that everyone should address. Electronic mail is not inherently a secure medium. It's not that hard to intercept a mail in transit, and delivery is not 100% assured. In addition eMail is easy to pass on, so it's easy for it to fall into the wrong hands.

In general, a good rule is never to put anything in an eMail which you wouldn't be happy to put on a postcard. A note to a colleague arranging a meeting is probably OK: a complaint about your boss, you should definitely think twice about. A fairly contentious issue is your credit card number.

Sending your credit card number over eMail is no more dangerous than giving it over the telephone, at least in general. There is a suggestion raised that it would be easy for a criminal to put a filter on a computer somewhere along the route from a to b, which scanned for credit card numbers (if you see the sequence "4929" there's a fair chance you've just found a Barclaycard number), and save them off. There's no evidence that this has actually happened yet, though. Fortunately, there are almost always ways of working round sending your credit card number.

A partial solution to the problem of confidentiality is to use encryption from one end to another. Several years ago there was a major row when the US tried to impose a hardware-based encryption system, using a chip to be placed in PCs called the "Clipper Chip". It just happened that Clipper-encoded documents could be freely decoded by the US government, you see. The outrage against this move was so great that the move was later cancelled. Netscape, and a number of other top-end WWW browsers provide "secure connections" to special (expensive) Web servers. This in theory allows you to enter financial or personal details without worrying that it could be intercepted.

For personal eMail, there is a system called "Pretty Good Privacy", or PGP for short. As the name implies, this is not the complete answer (MI5 would be able to decode your message, given time), but it's available free, and is quite widespread, and is adequate for most purposes. PGP allows you to use someone else's "key" to encrypt a message so that only they can decrypt it, and also allows you to use your key to "sign" a message so that it is proven that it came from you and that it hasn't been tampered with since you sent it. It allows you to hand out a "public key" without compromising the security of your own encryption. At the same time, you can use PGP to encrypt files on your own machine for your own use. There is an ongoing battle about the status of PGP. Its inventor, Phil Zimmerman, is currently being prosecuted for exporting US encryption secrets out of the USA. For this reason, you should never get the PGP software from a site on the US mainland. However, there are good archives available in the UK and in Europe, so the software is easy to acquire.

I've run PGP for a few years now, but I've never had the need to use it seriously, which is why I can't go into detail over how to use it. However, if you need encryption, it's worth looking at.

There have recently been scares that some forms of encryption, in particular Netscape's secure mode, have been cracked. This is less severe than it sounds, because breaking encryption for one connection does not automatically break any other, and most secure transactions only last for a few minutes. If it emerged that a Netscape secure transaction could be broken within a minute or two that would be a significant risk. At the moment it appears that the best efforts take a few hours. However, this is an issue which will not be sorted out completely for some time.

Viruses

Many people worry that if they connect to the Internet, their machine will become infected by viruses. This is only partially true.

The thing to remember is that despite occasional rumours to the contrary, you can only get a virus from an executable file - that is a .COM or an .EXE file. You can *not* contract viruses from eMails, news postings or from WWW pages, unless these have .EXE files attached, which you are then silly enough to run without checking first.

It is worth running virus checking software regularly. The type that run constantly, examining everything which goes onto your hard disk are useful in this case. However, viruses are pretty rare on the Internet - as soon as an infected file is identified, it is usually zapped before it can do any damage.

It's worth taking sensible precautions: in particular, only download files from large archives. These take special care to make sure that they are virus-free, and can in general be trusted. If someone you don't know sends you an executable file ("try this brilliant new game...") then treat it with great suspicion. Binaries posted to newsgroups (especially those posted to unexpected groups - that is, not to a binaries group) are also very suspicious.

I've said it once, but it's worth hammering in again: you can't get a virus from eMail. There's a warning which circles the Internet about the "Good Times" virus which supposedly is passed on through eMail. This is not true. The warning was posted as a joke, and has been wandering the Internet ever since. Pay no attention to it, and whatever you do, don't pass it on any further.

The Internet has its own sorts of viruses. A Windows PC on a dial-up link is not at risk from any of these, but I'll talk a bit about them because they're interesting.

The most famous Internet virus was the Internet Worm. Ironically the Worm was never intended to cause harm. It was an experiment to try and find out how big the Internet was, which went wrong. It was written by Robert T. Morris Jr, an ex-student of MIT, and was released on one of MIT's machines in late 1988.

When it ran, the Worm found all the machines to which the computer it was on was connected, and copied itself down the line to each of them. It then ran a copy of itself on each of these machines. It also reported back to base where it had been. All this would have been fine, except that Morris forgot to make the program check whether there was another copy of itself on a machine when it ran. Since most machines on the Internet were connected in one way or another to most other ones, there was rapidly a cascade, with computers all over the Internet passing copies of the Worm from one to another, which then created more copies, which then created more copies... The situation in the end was a bit like the end of the Sorcerer's Apprentice in Fantasia, with new copies of the Worm springing up faster than they could be stopped.

HANDY TIP

If you're really interested in protecting yourself from viruses, one of the best sources of information is the Internet. I'd recommend that you start with the newsgroup alt.virus and proceed from there.

The final effect of the Worm was to put the whole of the Internet out of action for about a day. I was on JANET, a network which had not yet been fully connected to the Internet at the time, so I was safe, but I remember the deathly silence from America that day. Morris was arrested and stood trial. There was some embarrassment when it was revealed that his father, Robert T. Morris Snr., was head of computer security for the US Government. There was also some debate as to where he should stand trial: he had run the program on a computer in Massachusetts, dialled in from a machine in New York, while he himself was physically in Florida - so where had he committed the crime? Eventually he was sentenced to community service for what he did.

The main reason the Worm was so successful at the time was that the Internet was almost entirely made up of two makes of computers: DEC VAXen and Sun Workstations. This is no longer the case, and it is believed that it is impossible for a Worm to attack the Internet today.

Hackers

I am one of the few fossils still remaining who resent the casual use of the word "hacker" to mean a person who breaks into computers. Originally a hacker was someone who "uses computers for the fun of it", with the implication of someone with a fair degree of skill. Someone who breaks into computers is properly referred to as a "cracker". However, the "H" word has entered public consciousness, so I must reluctantly follow suit.

First: Unless you run server programs on your machine, you can't be hacked, at least not directly (it is possible for hackers to break into your provider's computers, and maybe get at your eMail before you collect it, but that's their problem).

Second: Hacking is nowhere near as common, or as damaging, as is usually made out. Most hackers' methods are a good deal less exotic than are made out in films and in the press. For example, the best way to find passwords is "dumpster diving" - going through the waste bins outside a company when it's closed and finding all the notes where people have written down their passwords so they don't forget them.

If you'd like to try hacking yourself, then my first advice is don't. If you want to try anyway, be warned that it's a long, slow and fairly boring process, and there's a lot of more interesting material legitimately available. For example, NASA and the CIA were popular early targets: with the appearance of the World-Wide Web, and Al Gore's Open Government initiative, there's so much available anyway that it's not usually worth hacking.

Oh, and one last thing: any machine with *really* important information is going to be isolated from the Internet anyway!

Flame Wars

Moving on from the realms of the criminal, there are aspects of the Internet which we all encounter once in a while, and which can be disturbing the first time they are encountered. One of the more common (unfortunately) is the phenomenon of the "flame war".

One of the more interesting effects of eMail and News is that, while it is a much more immediate and emotional medium of communication than most forms of writing, many nuances of communication can get lost. It's often put forward as a great advantage that, "On the Internet nobody knows you're a dog", as a memorable cartoon once put it. This is true, but at the same time an awful lot of body language also disappears. In particular, emotions don't come over very well - regardless of whether you're joking, angry or sad, it all looks the same at the other end.

For this reason, a set of symbols have evolved in eMail called "emoticons", or "smileys" for short. The oldest of these, and the most well-known, is :-) - turn either your head or this book through 90 degrees to see what it means. There's a wide range of smileys, and there are even dictionaries of them, but very few of them actually get used - using too many smileys is thought of as a bit childish. The happy smiley is used to punctuate a sentence which is meant as a joke: The sad smiley :-(is used to show sadness or disappointment.

Even when using smileys, it's easy for misunderstandings to arise, largely because the combination of immediacy and distance mean that it's very tempting to get overly personal with people. On receiving a critical eMail, or reading a post critical of you, the first impulse is to reply with something equally direct and personal. After all, it only takes a minute to write a reply, and then you can press the send button and it's gone.

This is a mistake. A flame, as a personally critical message is known, provokes a flame in return - only worse. For some reason, it never occurs to the person who sent the original flame, that it might just be because he'd been unreasonable that suddenly everyone was being so unreasonable to him. So he, in turn, responds.... Soon the original topic of discussion has become hopelessly lost in a sea of "Well, my dad always used to say..." and "It should be perfectly obvious to any intelligent person that...," and eventually there is nothing left but direct personal insults which get more and more extreme until finally both sides lose interest. Comparisons to the House of Commons or tabloid newspapers are totally appropriate here.

The first time you encounter a flame war, assuming you're lucky enough to be a participant, it's quite exciting. The ninth time is less fun, and just uses up lots of bandwidth which could otherwise be used to discuss the matter at hand. Take it from me, the first time you're the *victim* of a flame, it feels awful. For the record, I was first flamed some time in 1987, over some details of the personnel of Thunderbirds. Yeah, it was that important. It still felt like the end of the world to me.

The best way to avoid flame wars is to stop before you send that eMail or that posting and ask yourself "is this contributing to the discussion? Would I say this to my mother/best friend/boss? Are there any spelling mistakes? (If there are, they will be picked up on relentlessly.) Does my argument hold water? Are the facts correct? Do I really want to go through all of this?". If not, then no matter how much you want to make the point, discard the message. You know it makes sense.

There are those out there who take delight in picking on beginners ("newbies" as they refer to them) and flaming them, even when they've asked a sensible question. This is why I emphasised that you should read a group for a while before posting. All you can do with these people is to reflect on what sad lives they lead. But this brings us on to...

Trolls

A troll is a posting deliberately intended to provoke a flame war. At first sight this seems like a pretty silly thing to do, but some people delight in it, and in a newsgroup which has a group of regulars plus a collection of newcomers, it can end up as something of a running joke. Part of the reason for this section is to warn you of some of the classic trolls, so that you can be ready when you see them, and won't rush to the bait.

The term "troll" is said to come from fishing: "trolling" is casting a bait a long way out and pulling it slowly back in order to attract the fish to your boat. In a similar way, a troll will garner a collection of newbies who can then be gently taken to pieces. Sometimes, leave out the "gently".

The classic troll is "What does the 'T' stand for in 'James T. Kirk'?". The answer, if you really want to know, is "Tiberius" (in "The Wrath of Khan" it was carved on his gravestone). This is a pretty obscure bit of information, and there are plenty of people who are very proud of themselves for knowing it. So, if someone comes along who insists until they're blue in the face that it stands for "Tracy" you'd want to put him right pronto, right? Wrong. That's what they want. For what it's worth, many people on Usenet agree that it really stands for "Troll", regardless of what the film says.

Some trolls are less stylised. Any posting to uk.misc (or, for that matter, to most groups) which is either strongly pro-vegetarian or pro-carnivore will definitely provoke a fight which should last for a couple of months. Now, I'm not saying that anyone would post a provocative message on this topic *deliberately*, but the fact that there is more-or-less always a row about just this subject on uk.misc does look suspicious.

My favourite troll occurred on the group covering the TV series Twin Peaks, during the time that the series was first on in the USA. One week the TV network cancelled the show without warning, showing sport instead. Someone posted a message asking if this was the same all over the country. Someone else replied "Oh, didn't you see it? It was great!" and continued to recount a series of imagined events which had occurred in that episode. Other people joined in, and the descriptions grew more and more baroque as the week went on. At one point someone tried to blow the whistle and point out that the alleged episode never existed, and someone else replied: "Just because you missed it you're trying to suggest that it never existed!" After a week, the series continued with no interruption, and the "missing episode" entered the annals of Usenet legend.

Forewarned is Forearmed

This section looks at a couple of traps for the Internet beginner which don't regularly fit into any other category. None of these will actually cause you harm (though they might get you flamed), but you should know about them, so that when you encounter them you'll know what you're dealing with.

KIBO

James "KIBO" Parry is a typographer who lives and works in Boston, Massachusetts. This is about all that is known about him in real life.

Kibo is noted on the Internet because he has programs running on his computer which scan the whole of Usenet looking for occurrences of the word "Kibo" (or any of the obvious variations). Anything he sees, he replies to.

The effect of this in practice is that any mention of his name anywhere on Usenet causes Kibo to pop up - a bit like in the film "Beetlejuice", when you said his name and he appeared.

Beyond that, Kibo is pretty harmless. He is noted for having a signature file which is over 10 pages long, which he sometimes posts as a joke, but he's usually pretty kind to beginners.

Oh yes, and there's a rumour around that KIBO stands for "knowledge in, bullshit out" - but you didn't hear it from me.

Craig Shergold

At some point or other, one of your contacts on the Internet will send you a copy of the following sob story: "Little Craig Shergold has leukaemia. His dying wish is to get into the Guinness Book of Records as the recipient of the largest number of get-well-soon cards. Please send little Craig a card at....".

As far as it goes, this story is perfectly true. What it doesn't mention, however, is that Craig is now in his late teens, responded to treatment well and is now totally cured. The Maundsley hospital, where he was treated, would really like to have back the room which is set aside to store all the mailbags of get-well cards which arrive every day. In recent years the request has transmuted into postcards and business cards, too.

What happened was this: The request was originally completely genuine, and at some point found its way to someone who had an eMail account, who decided to do Craig a good turn by sending it to his friends. They in turn forwarded the message to their friends, who passed it on, until today it wanders the Internet like some strange electronic flying Dutchman.

Nip it in the bud. It won't do any good, though - the message seems to re-emerge about every nine months regardless of what anyone does.

There is a similar bogus story going around about Niemann-Marcus chocolate chip cookies. The story goes like this: a lady (whose identity is lost in the mists of time) was having coffee in Niemann-Marcus' coffee shop, and was very taken by their chocolate chip cookies. She asked for the recipe: sure they said, but we'll have to charge you for it. "How much?" "Two-fifty." "OK, put it on my bill."

When she received her next credit card bill, she found that she'd been charged $250 dollars instead of $2.50. It turned out that this was indeed the cost, and Niemann-Marcus wouldn't refund her money. She was so incensed that she passed the recipe on to everyone she knew, asking them to pass it in turn. You can guess the rest...

This story is still going strong on the Internet, and was even reported in The Times as a genuine news story in September 1995 (about a week after The Times' own computer editor had revealed it as false, as it happens).

Again, if you receive this message, do not pass it on. However, it is worth trying the recipe. I don't eat chocolate, but I'm told that it does make rather good cookies. Oh, and there is *no* truth in the rumour at all - apparently, Niemann-Marcus don't make their own chocolate chip cookies.

MAKE MONEY FAST

Once in a while, you may receive a message like this: the original one had a Subject line of MAKE MONEY FAST all in capitals.

The message contains a list of names and addresses, and tells you to send $1 (or the equivalent in your currency) to each of the people on the list. Then remove the top name on the list, add your own, and mail it on to six people you know.

It's a chain letter, just like you sometimes get through the post. These are illegal in most countries. Whatever you do, don't send any money. Do not pass it on to anyone. Delete it. Simple as that.

Spamming (Case Study: Cantor and Siegal)

With any luck, the story of Cantor and Siegal won't be repeated on the Internet. However, the Internet is not the luckiest of places...

Cantor and Siegal were a firm of US lawyers who went in for one of the less nice legal scams in recent years. It's not very well-known that the United States runs a Green Card lottery every year: anyone can go along to the US embassy, fill in a card with their name and address, and every year or so they make a draw and the few people whose cards are drawn (from the thousands submitted) are given a Green Card - that is, full US citizenship. In the last few years, some firms of lawyers have exploited this by offering their services to "help you get US citizenship" - that is, they will charge you £100 to fill in a card for you and put it in on your behalf. You sometimes see adverts for these services in the small ads in the back of newspapers.

Cantor and Siegal took this to extremes, by putting out their advert on the Internet. In particular, they sent a copy to every single newsgroup. This behaviour is known casually as "spamming" and is frowned on. Boy, is it frowned on.

There are two normal responses to spams: first, and more responsibly, complain to their Internet provider or system administrator. This happened in this case. Second is what's known as "mail-bombing". If you look around on the hard disk of your PC, it's not that hard to find a large meaningless file. It's fairly easy to attach this to an eMail. On certain Internet-connected systems, it's not very hard to set the system up so that it mails a couple of hundred of these eMails-wrapped-round-a-brick back to the perpetrators of the spam.

This is what happened to Cantor and Siegal. The volume of abusive eMail was so much that their Internet provider crashed under the strain, and was put out of action for several days. Not surprisingly, the providers promptly cancelled C&S's account, and sued them for damages for all the trouble they'd caused.

Let this be a lesson for us all.

Legal Issues

The Internet gives you a great feeling that everything is available, and that nothing is illegal. This is only partially true.

There are police in the UK who are experienced in Internet-based crime. Their attitude is that while they don't mind people reading sex newsgroups, there are some activities which go on which are definite crimes (trafficking in pornography, for example), and they will pursue them in the same way as they would any conventional crime.

In general you are no more or less safe from arrest or prosecution if you commit a crime using the Internet than if you use telephones or the Post Office.

A related issue is the liability of your provider should you commit a crime. This is still in some doubt. In the USA, the Church of Scientology is not only suing one of its ex-members for breach of copyright (apparently the doctrines of the church are copyright) but they are also suing his Internet provider. The result of the case will not be known for some time.

Pornography!

Every few weeks, you read in the papers about all this pornography which is to be found on the Internet. Well, yes, to a degree, it's true. There is pornography on the Internet. There are 40 million people, so there's a bit of more-or-less everything on the Internet.

However, don't expect to be instantly swamped by this tide of filth. There is some quite extreme stuff out there, but it's quite well hidden and you'll probably have to pay for it, too. Of the stuff which is easily available, when interviewed by the press, I always say that a copy of Playboy in W.H. Smiths is cheaper, easier to get hold of, and more revealing. Actually, a copy of Marie Claire will probably be cheaper, easier to get hold of and more revealing.

A more significant worry is if you've got children yourself and are worried about exposing them to all this.

There are self-regulation schemes appearing on the Internet which give sites and pages "certificates" rather like a film. There are commercial packages available, such as Net Nanny, which will limit access based on this certification (though very few sites are certificated at all). Microsoft Internet Explorer has this filtering system built-in. There are also packages available which filter input depending on dubious words or addresses. Personally, I'm dubious as to how well these systems work.

At the end of the day, there's nothing which will stop a determined and intelligent thirteen-year-old from finding dubious material. Filters and suchlike can do a certain amount, but in the end it comes down to educating your kids as to what is and is not acceptable.

CHAPTER TEN

Where to Find Internet Software

All the software that has been described in this book can be downloaded from the Internet. This chapter brings together a list of the sites to visit to find the packages.

Covers

Introduction

The Internet is developing at an astounding rate. One effect of this is that software is constantly being upgraded, and new products are appearing all the time. Whereas you would only expect new versions of a word processor or a spreadsheet every year or so, it's quite normal for there to be new versions of Internet software every few weeks. This can seem pretty alarming at first, but it's one of those things about the Internet that you should be prepared for and learn to get used to.

During the time that I've been writing this book, there have been new versions of most of the software that I describe. I've tried as far as I can to use the latest versions that I can get hold of, but it's inevitable that by the time you read this book some of these will not be the latest versions. Therefore, in this chapter I describe how to download the latest version of all the Internet software used in this book.

General Servers

There are a number of sites on the Internet where you will find all the software I have mentioned in one place. This is less trouble than going to each individual site, but remember that you may not get documentation files etc., and sometimes the versions are out of date.

A useful first place to look for software is "**Shareware.com**". Point your browser at **http:// www.shareware.com/** to find the site. You can search for software by name or by function, and it will then list the nearest FTP site for you to download the software from.

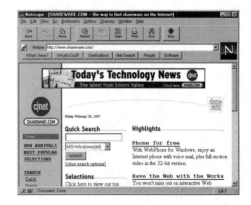

Shareware.com is run by the C-Net on-line service, so there is a range of other services available - news, reviews and articles.

If you run Windows 95 you should *definitely* check out **"Windows95.com"**, which can be found at **http://www.windows95.com/**. This site is actually

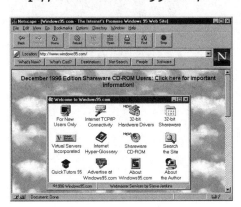

independent of Microsoft, but despite this, it appears to have absolutely *everything* for Windows 95. Besides the Internet software, there's all that 32-bit shareware they tell you about, news, tutorials and much more.

Trumpet Winsock

If you don't have a TCP/IP stack at all, then you won't be able to fetch this software, so it's academic as to where to get it. If you don't run Windows 95, the best shareware TCP/IP stack is Trumpet Winsock. You can find the latest version at **http://www.trumpet.com.au**

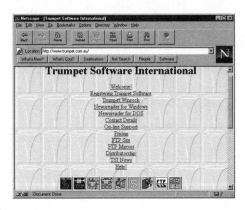

Netscape/Internet Explorer

Netscape's home page is at **http://home.netscape.com**. If you're running Netscape, finding the home page is easy: simply click on the "N" icon in the top-right-hand corner, and you go there. Besides new versions of the software, Netscape have instructions on how to get the most from

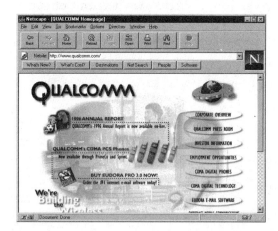

Netscape, site lists, and lots more.

Microsoft's Web site carries similar material relating to its own browser: download Internet Explorer from **http://www.microsoft.com/ie/**.

Eudora

The eMail program Eudora is produced by Qualcomm Inc. Full up-to-date information on both the free and paid-for versions is to be found at their home page, **http://www.qualcomm.com**. It's worth checking out because you can find MS Word versions of the official Eudora manuals there, too.

Agent

Look at Forte Inc.'s home page, **http://www.forteinc.com/** to download the Usenet news-reader Free Agent, or to buy the commercial version, Agent.

WS FTP

The author of WS FTP is John Junod. His home page always has the latest version available. You can find it at **http://www.csra.net/junodj/**

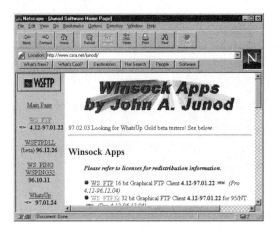

Ewan

Peter Zander, the author of the Telnet terminal emulator Ewan, keeps a home page for it at **http://www.varg.lysator.liu.se/~zander/ewan.html**.

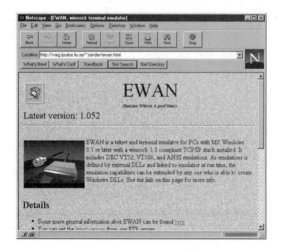

mIRC

The main mIRC site is found at **http://www.mirc.co.uk**. You can download the program from there, and find a wide range of information on using it.

There are "mirrors" (local copies) of the site around the world - even one in Brazil!

Index